3

GOVERNMENT PROCEDURES AND OPERATIONS

THE FISCAL STRAINS ON STATE GOVERNMENTS

GOVERNMENT PROCEDURES AND OPERATIONS

Additional books in this series can be found on Nova's website under the Series tab.

Additional E-books in this series can be found on Nova's website under the E-books tab.

ECONOMIC ISSUES, PROBLEMS AND PERSPECTIVES

Additional books in this series can be found on Nova's website under the Series tab.

Additional E-books in this series can be found on Nova's website under the E-books tab.

GOVERNMENT PROCEDURES AND OPERATIONS

THE FISCAL STRAINS ON STATE GOVERNMENTS

ARTHUR HORVÁTH
EDITOR

Nova Science Publishers, Inc.
New York

For permission to use material from this book please contact us:
Telephone 631-231-7269; Fax 631-231-8175
Web Site: http://www.novapublishers.com

Library of Congress Cataloging-in-Publication Data

The fiscal strains on state governments / editors, Arthur Horvath.
p. cm.
Includes index.
ISBN 978-1-62100-046-4 (softcover)
1. Finance, Public--United States--States. 2. Local finance--United States--States. 3. Grants-in-aid--United States. 4. Debts, Public--United States--States. I. Horvath, Arthur.
HJ275.F5585 2011
336'.01373--dc23
2011030093

Published by Nova Science Publishers, Inc. † New York

CONTENTS

PREFACE

States have different budget cycles, different ways of preparing revenue estimates and forecasts, different requirements concerning their operating and capital budgets, different roles for their governors in the budget process, and different policies concerning the carrying over of operating budget deficits into the next fiscal year. Although no two state budgets are alike, all fifty states experienced heightened levels of fiscal stress during FY2009 and FY2010. The national economic recession, which officially lasted from December 2007 to June 2009, led to lower levels of economic activity throughout the nation and reduced state tax revenues. This book examines the current status of state fiscal conditions and the role of federal assistance in state budgets. It begins with a brief overview of state budgeting procedures and then provides budgetary data comparing state fiscal conditions in FY2008 to FY2010.

Chapter 1 - No two state budgets are alike. States have different budget cycles, different ways of preparing revenue estimates and forecasts, different requirements concerning their operating and capital budgets, different roles for their governors in the budget process, and different policies concerning the carrying over of operating budget deficits into the next fiscal year.

Chapter 2 - The financial consequences of the recession that spanned from December 2007 through June 2009 have increased congressional interest in the financial health of state and local governments. State and local tax revenues declined, expenditures climbed, and debt increased. Even though tax revenue has begun to rebound, expenditures for unemployment benefits and other social programs remain elevated. Also, federal aid to states, which had increased as part of the American Recovery and Reinvestment Act, has begun to recede. Federal outlays for grants in aid to state and local governments rose from $538 billion in FY2009 to $608.4 billion in FY2010 and are estimated to be $625.2 billion in FY2011. The FY2012 budget provides $584.3 billion in outlays for aid to state and local governments in 2012.

Chapter 3 - As you know well, the deep recession of 2008 through 2009 and the subsequent slow recovery have battered state and local budgets. As the recession took hold, revenues dropped precipitously, especially at the state level. Driven partly by balanced-budget requirements under their constitutions, many governments have responded by cutting numerous programs and reducing workforces. As necessary as these cuts may have been, they have left some jurisdictions struggling to maintain essential services. The fiscal problems of state and local governments have also had national implications, as their spending cuts and tax increases have been a headwind on the economic recovery. Moreover, concerns about both the current fiscal condition of these governments and their longer-term commitments to provide pensions and health benefits have recently led to strains in municipal bond markets.

In: The Fiscal Strains on State Governments ISBN: 978-1-62100-046-4
Editor: Arthur Horváth

Chapter 1

STATE GOVERNMENT FISCAL STRESS AND FEDERAL ASSISTANCE

Robert Jay Dilger

SUMMARY

No two state budgets are alike. States have different budget cycles, different ways of preparing revenue estimates and forecasts, different requirements concerning their operating and capital budgets, different roles for their governors in the budget process, and different policies concerning the carrying over of operating budget deficits into the next fiscal year.

Although no two state budgets are alike, all 50 states experienced heightened levels of fiscal stress during FY2009 and FY2010. The national economic recession, which officially lasted from December 2007 to June 2009, led to lower levels of economic activity throughout the nation and reduced state tax revenues. State tax revenues from all sources, including sales, personal, and corporate income tax collections, fell from $680.2 billion in FY2008 to an estimated $609.7 billion in FY2010, a decline of 10.4%. The decline in state tax revenue, coupled with state-balanced operating budget requirements, created what the National Association of State Budget Officers (NASBO) characterized as "one of the worst time periods in state fiscal conditions since the Great Depression." For example, even with an additional $107 billion in temporary federal assistance provided through P.L. 111-5, the

American Recovery and Reinvestment Act of 2009 (ARRA) in FY2010, states reduced their general fund expenditures by 7.3% from FY2009 ($660.9 billion) to FY2010 ($612.6 billion), enacted $23.9 billion in increased taxes and fees, and raised an additional $7.5 billion through other revenue measures. Although state tax revenue for FY2011 and FY2012 are projected to be above FY2010 levels, state budget officers predict continuing budgetary challenges in virtually all states in FY2011 and FY2012.

Congressional interest in state budgetary finances has increased in recent years, primarily because state action to address budget shortfalls, such as increasing taxes, laying off or furloughing state employees, and postponing or eliminating state infrastructure projects, could have an adverse affect on the national economic recovery. For example, Federal Reserve Board Chairman, Benjamin Bernanke, stated on March 2, 2011, that the fiscal problems of state and local governments have "had national implications, as their spending cuts and tax increases have been a headwind on the economic recovery." Also, if states reduce their service levels there could be additional pressure for the federal government to provide those services. Moreover, as funding from ARRA expires, there could be additional pressure for the federal government to provide additional federal assistance to states.

This report examines the current status of state fiscal conditions and the role of federal assistance in state budgets. It begins with a brief overview of state budgeting procedures and then provides budgetary data comparing state fiscal conditions in FY2008 to FY2010. The data presented in this report indicate that (1) states cut their general fund budgets from FY2008 to FY2010, but, because they received increased federal funding, increased their total amount of spending; (2) the share of total state expenditures held by the states' four operating expenditures budgets (general fund, federal funds, other state funds, and bonds) shifted from FY2008 to FY2010, with an increased reliance on federal funds; and (3) states experienced varying levels of fiscal stress from FY2008 to FY2010. This report concludes with an assessment of the consequences current levels of state fiscal stress may have for the 112th Congress.

State Budgets

No two state budgets are alike.[1] For example, 27 states have an annual budget cycle, 21 states have a biennial budget cycle, and 2 states have an annual budget cycle for some agencies or purposes and a biennial budget cycle for others.[2] Most states (46) begin their fiscal year on July 1, 2 states begin their fiscal year on October 1 (Alabama and Michigan), 1 state begins its fiscal year on September 1 (Texas), and 1 state begins its fiscal year on April 1(New York).[3]

States also have different ways of preparing their revenue estimates and forecasts that project the amount of revenue that will be available based on current law to support operating costs and capital outlays in the current and future fiscal years. These revenue estimates are important because they establish the general parameters for the state's budget at the outset of the budget process.[4] The state budget office is solely responsible for revenue forecasting in 13 states, a board or commission is solely responsible in 11 states, and the state revenue office is solely responsible in 3 states. The remaining states use a combination of agencies or boards to develop their revenue forecasts.[5]

All but one state (Vermont) has some form of a balanced operating budget requirement, either in statute or in their state constitution, but the stringency of these requirements vary, ranging from having only a requirement that the governor submit a balanced operating budget for the legislature's consideration (2 states) to having a prohibition against carrying a deficit forward and requirements that the governor propose, the legislature pass, and the governor sign a balanced operating budget (26 states).[6] Overall, governors in 44 states must submit a balanced operating budget for legislative consideration, state legislatures in 41 states must pass a balanced operating budget, the governor must sign a balanced operating budget in 37 states, and 43 states have a prohibition against carrying a operating budget deficit forward.[7] Also, the extent of the governor's authority in the budget process varies among the states. The governor can spend unanticipated federal funds in 30 states, reduce enacted budgets in 38 states, veto an item within the appropriations bill in 41 states, veto selected words in 15 states, and use the veto to change the meaning of words in 4 states.[8]

Although 43 states have a prohibition against carrying a operating budget deficit forward, all states incur debt to finance capital projects, typically subject to limits on debt service (31 states), levels of authorized debt (44 states), or both (29 states).[9] State government long-term debt was $1.038 trillion at the end of FY2009, an increase of 4.8% from FY2008.[10]

Although no two state budgets are alike, all 50 states experienced heightened levels of fiscal stress during FY2009 and FY2010.[11] The national economic recession, which officially lasted from December 2007 to June 2009, led to lower levels of economic activity throughout the nation and reduced state tax revenues. State tax revenues from all sources, including sales, personal, and corporate income tax collections, fell from $680.2 billion in FY2008 to an estimated $609.7 billion in FY2010, a decline of 10.4%.[12] The decline in state tax revenue, coupled with state-balanced operating budget requirements, created what the National Association of State Budget Officers (NASBO) characterized as "one of the worst time periods in state fiscal conditions since the Great Depression."[13] For example, even with an additional $107 billion in temporary federal assistance provided through P.L. 111-5, the American Recovery and Reinvestment Act of 2009 (ARRA) in FY2010, states reduced their general fund expenditures by 7.3% from FY2009 ($660.9 billion) to FY2010 ($612.6 billion), enacted $23.9 billion in increased taxes and fees, and raised an additional $7.5 billion through other revenue measures.[14]

State budget officers predict continuing budgetary challenges in virtually all states in FY2011 and FY2012. They note that "state revenues are forecast to remain well below their pre-recession 2008 levels" and that "a significant amount of state funding made available by the American Recovery and Reinvestment Act of 2009 will no longer be available."[15] In addition, projected costs for Medicaid, state employee pension and retirement health care obligations, and delayed infrastructure projects are also expected to provide continuing budgetary challenges for states.[16]

Congressional interest in state budgetary finances has increased in recent years, primarily because state action to address budget shortfalls, such as increasing taxes, laying off or furloughing state employees, and postponing or eliminating state infrastructure projects, could have an adverse affect on the national economic recovery. For example, Federal Reserve Board Chairman, Benjamin Bernanke, stated on March 2, 2011, that the fiscal problems of state and local governments have "had national implications, as their spending cuts and tax increases have been a headwind on the economic recovery."[17] Also, if states reduce their service levels there could be additional pressure for the federal government to provide those services. Moreover, as funding from ARRA expires, there could be additional pressure for the federal government to provide additional federal assistance to states.

This report examines the current status of state fiscal conditions and the role of federal assistance in state budgets. It begins with a brief overview of state budgeting procedures and then provides budgetary data comparing state fiscal conditions in FY2008 to FY2010. As will be discussed, the data presented in this report indicate that (1) states cut their general fund budgets from FY2008 to FY2010, but, because they received increased federal funding, increased their total amount of spending; (2) the share of total state expenditures held by the states' four operating expenditures budgets (general fund, federal funds, other state funds, and bonds) shifted from FY2008 to FY2010, with an increased reliance on federal funds; and (3) states experienced varying levels of fiscal stress from FY2008 to FY2010. This report concludes with an assessment of the consequences current levels of state fiscal stress may have for the 112th Congress.

STATE BUDGETARY PROCEDURES

Unlike the federal government, states budget separately for current operating expenditures and for capital expenditures. As mentioned previously, virtually all states (except Vermont) have some form of a balanced operating budget requirement, and most states have restrictions on the amount of debt that they issue to finance capital projects.[18]

Current State Operating Expenditures

Most states account for their current operating expenditures through four budgets:

- the *state general fund budget* refers to expenditures from revenues accruing to the state from taxes, fees, interest earnings, and other sources which can be used for the general operation of state government.
- the *state federal funds budget* refers to expenditures from funds received directly from the federal government.
- the *other state funds budget* refers to expenditures from revenue sources that are restricted by law for particular governmental functions or activities; for example, a gasoline tax dedicated to a state highway trust fund would appear in other state funds.
- the *state bonds budget* refers to expenditures from the sale of bonds, generally for capital projects.[19]

Also, 48 states (Kansas and Montana are the exceptions) have a state budget stabilization fund, budget reserve account, or "rainy day" fund to cover unanticipated revenue shortfalls.[20] The amount of revenue set aside in these funds vary from state-to-state, generally ranging from 3% to 10% of appropriations.[21] In recent years, state end-of-year balances, which include ending balances and budget stabilization, budget reserve account, and "rainy day" funds, have declined from 8.6% of total state expenditures in FY2008 to 6.4% in FY2010 (2.4% in FY2010 if Alaska and Texas are excluded).[22] Most budget analysts suggest as an "informal rule-of-thumb" that states set aside at least 5% of expenditures for unanticipated budget shortfalls.[23] In FY2010, 28 states had end-of-year balances below the recommended amount and 32 states anticipate having end-of-year balances below the recommended amount in FY2011.[24]

The State Capital Budget

The state capital budget is associated with the acquisition or construction of major capital projects, including land, buildings, structures, and major equipment. Minor repairs and routine maintenance are typically reported as operating expenses. Funds for capital projects traditionally has come primarily from non-general fund sources. In FY2009, funds for capital projects came from dedicated fees and surpluses (35.1% in FY2009), bonds (32.5% in FY2009), federal funds (26.5% in FY2009), and state general funds/end-of-year operating surpluses (5.9% in FY2009).[25]

State capital spending totaled $80.3 billion in FY2008, $84.2 billion in FY2009, and an estimated $88.8 billion in FY2010.[26] According to NASBO, the increase in state capital spending since FY2008 is at least partly due to increased federal funding provided by ARRA and several ARRA bond provisions, such as Build America Bonds, Recovery Zone Economic Development Bonds, and School Construction Bonds.[27] In FY2009, transportation projects accounted for 56.8% ($47.8 billion) of all state capital expenditures, followed by higher education projects at 12.2% ($10.3 billion), environmental projects at 7.0% ($5.9 billion), corrections projects at 2.2% ($1.81 billion), housing projects at 1.3% ($1.1 billion) and other capital projects, such as public school facilities, zoo improvements, health care infrastructure, and sports facilities, at 20.5% ($17.3 billion).[28]

TRENDS IN STATE EXPENDITURES

This section examines trends in state expenditures, in nominal dollars, from FY2008 to FY2010, starting with total state expenditures (including the states' capital budgets) and followed by each of the states' four operating expenditures budgets (state general fund, federal funds, other state funds, and bonds). FY2008 is used as the starting point for comparative purposes in most of the discussion because FY2008 is currently being used by many in Congress as the baseline for making comparisons in current federal budget debates.[29]

Three general conclusions can be drawn from the data presented in the following tables. First, states cut their general fund budgets from FY2008 to FY2010, but increased their total amount of spending. Faced with declining own-source revenue, states cut their general fund budgets by $60.7 billion from FY2008 to FY2010. However, because expenditures from the states' federal funds budgets increased by $175.5 billion from FY2008 to FY2010, and expenditures from other state funds budgets ($21.7 billion) and state bonds budgets ($9.4 billion) also increased, total state expenditures increased by $145.9 billion from FY2008 to FY2010. Media reports of recent state budget cuts and reports of the need for states to make future budget cuts typically refer to the states' general fund budgets or to budget cuts necessary to maintain current service levels, not to total state expenditures. The possible implications for Congress, and for the states, of the projected decrease in state federal assistance over the next several years is discussed later in this report.

Second, as shown in Figure 1, the share of total state expenditures held by the states' four operating expenditures budgets shifted from FY2008 to FY2010, with an increased reliance on federal funds. For example, in FY2008, the states' general fund budgets accounted for 45.9% of total state spending, their federal funds budgets accounted for 26.3%, their other state funds budgets accounted for 25.5%, and their bonds budgets accounted for 2.3%. In FY2010, the states' general fund budgets accounted for 38.1% of total state spending, their federal funds budgets accounted for 34.7%, their other state funds budgets accounted for 24.5%, and their bonds budgets accounted for 2.7%.[30] The possible implications for Congress, and for the states, of the states' increased reliance on federal funds is discussed later in this report.

Third, the data suggest that states experienced varying levels of fiscal stress from FY2008 to FY2010. For example, if state fiscal stress had been evenly distributed, the change in total state expenditures and the change in state general fund expenditures from FY2008 to FY2010 would have been expected to be fairly evenly distributed across states. However, the change in total state expenditures varied across the states, ranging from a reduction of $9.796 billion in North Carolina to an increase of $23.566 billion in California. Overall, from FY2008 to FY2010, 4 states reduced their total expenditures and 46 increased their total expenditures. Also, the change in state general fund expenditures also varied across the states, ranging from a reduction of $16.5 billion in California to an increase of $2.9 billion in Texas. Overall, from FY2008 to FY2010, 9 states increased their general fund expenditures and 41 states cut their general fund expenditures.

The variation in state fiscal stress experienced from FY2008 to FY2010 is typical of state responses to past national economic downturns. As the Government Accountability Office (GAO) has reported, "revenue fluctuations during national recessions vary substantially across states ... due in part to states' differing tax structures, economic conditions, and industrial bases."[31]

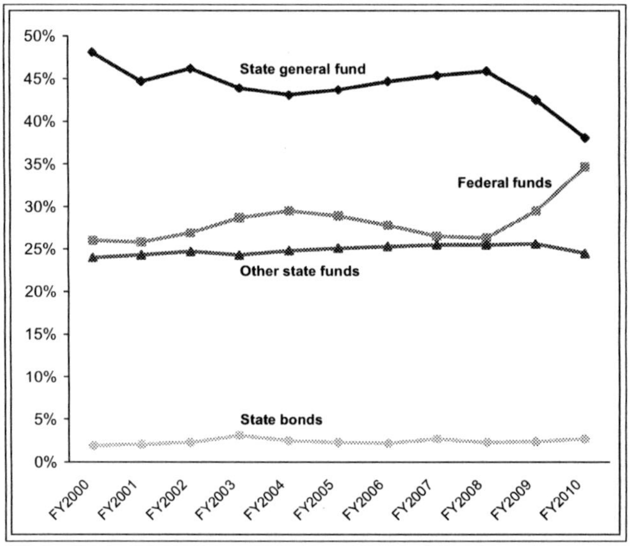

Source: National Association of State Budget Officers, *State Expenditure Report [various fiscal years]*, Washington, DC, all p. 2, *http://www.nasbo.org* /Publications/StateExpenditureReport/StateExpenditureReportArchives/ tabid/107/Default.aspx.

Note: FY2010 total state expenditures and share from the state general fund, federal funds, other state funds, and state bonds are estimated from state budget documents.

Figure 1. Total State Expenditures for FY2000-FY2010, by Funding Source (% of total state expenditures).

Also, unemployment rates have varied across states during both the most recent and past recessions and GAO has found that "while economic downturns within states generally occur around the same time as national recessions, their timing—or entrance into and exit out of the economic downturn—and duration varies."[32] The implications for Congress of these variations in state fiscal stress, as well as various ways to measure state fiscal stress, are discussed later in this report.

Table 1. Total State Expenditures (Capital Inclusive), FY2000-FY2010 ($ in millions)

FY	Total Amount of State Expenditures	Change in Total Amount of State Expenditures from Previous FY	% Change in Total Amount of State Expenditures from Previous FY
2000	$946,086	$65,834	7.48%
2001	$1,015,813	$69,727	7.37%
2002	$1,088,207	$72,394	7.13%
2003	$1,127,261	$39,054	3.59%
2004	$1,181,330	$54,069	4.80%
2005	$1,266,396	$85,066	7.20%
2006	$1,343,118	$76,722	6.06%
2007	$1,425,028	$81,910	6.10%
2008	$1,478,782	$53,754	3.77%
2009	$1,546,804	$68,022	4.60%
2010 est.	$1,624,666	$77,862	5.03%

Source: National Association of State Budget Officers, various FY State Expenditure Reports, Washington, DC, from FY2000-FY2009, all p. 6, *http://nasbo.org /Publications/StateExpenditureReport/StateExpenditureReportArchives/tabid/107/ Default.aspx.*

Total State Expenditures

As shown in Table 1, total state expenditures (capital inclusive) increased every fiscal year from FY2000 through FY2010, ranging from an increase of $39,054 million in FY2003 to $85,066 million in FY2005. In percentage terms, total state expenditures increased, on average, by 6.52% from FY2000 to FY2010, ranging from 3.59% in FY2003 to 7.48% in FY2000.

Table 2. Change in Total State Expenditures, FY2008-FY2010 ($ in millions)

State	Total State Expenditures, FY2008	Total State Expenditures, FY2010	Change in Total State Expenditures, FY2008 to FY2010
Alabama	$19,840	$24,458	$4,618
Alaska	$11,656	$9,746	-$1,910
Arizona	$25,247	$27,511	$2,264
Arkansas	$16,899	$20,249	$3,350
California	$194,276	$217,842	$23,566
Colorado	$25,129	$29,003	$3,874
Connecticut	$24,270	$26,062	$1,792
Delaware	$8,621	$8,720	$99
Florida	$64,379	$66,505	$2,126
Georgia	$38,494	$38,621	$127
Hawaii	$11,160	$10,948	-$212
Idaho	$5,932	$7,130	$1,198
Illinois	$44,566	$47,426	$2,860
Indiana	$24,239	$26,662	$2,423
Iowa	$16,129	$18,546	$2,417
Kansas	$12,689	$14,497	$1,808
Kentucky	$22,995	$25,837	$2,842
Louisiana	$28,888	$29,612	$724
Maine	$7,427	$8,257	$830
Maryland	$30,408	$33,409	$3,001
Massachusetts	$43,807	$53,410	$9,603
Michigan	$43,982	$45,723	$1,741
Minnesota	$28,446	$31,502	$3,056
Mississippi	$15,539	$19,384	$3,845
Missouri	$21,432	$24,811	$3,379
Montana	$5,357	$6,049	$692
Nebraska	$8,711	$9,591	$880
Nevada	$9,240	$7,875	-$1,365
New Hampshire	$4,807	$5,465	$658
New Jersey	$48,704	$48,975	$271
New Mexico	$14,207	$14,351	$144
New York	$116,056	$130,937	$14,881

State	Total State Expenditures, FY2008	Total State Expenditures, FY2010	Change in Total State Expenditures, FY2008 to FY2010
North Carolina	$41,588	$31,792	-$9,796
North Dakota	$3,597	$4,710	$1,113
Ohio	$56,763	$57,640	$877
Oklahoma	$20,730	$21,559	$829
Oregon	$22,174	$27,920	$5,746
Pennsylvania	$58,696	$70,376	$11,680
Rhode Island	$7,118	$8,162	$1,044
South Carolina	$20,787	$22,567	$1,780
South Dakota	$3,217	$3,769	$552
Tennessee	$26,033	$29,136	$3,103
Texas	$81,097	$97,867	$16,770
Utah	$11,323	$12,927	$1,604
Vermont	$5,308	$5,822	$514
Virginia	$35,330	$40,773	$5,443
Washington	$31,732	$32,543	$811
West Virginia	$18,710	$20,247	$1,537
Wisconsin	$36,089	$40,085	$3,996
Wyoming	$4,958	$7,657	$2,699
Total	$1,478,782	$1,624,666	$145,884

Source: CRS computations from National Association of State Budget Officers, FY2009 State Expenditure Report, Washington, DC, p. 6, *http://nasbo.org/LinkClick.aspx?fileticket=%2bPqnl4oZw2I%3d&tabid=79.*

Notes: Total state expenditures includes expenditures from the state's general fund account, federal funds account, other state funds, and bonds. FY2010 total state expenditures are estimated from state budget documents.

The percentage increase in total state expenditures in FY2009 (4.60%) and FY2010 (5.03%) were below the average for the time period.

As shown in Table 2, total state expenditures (capital inclusive) increased by more than $145 billion from FY2008 to FY2010 (from $1,478,782 million in FY2008 to $1,624,666 million in FY2010). Four states (Alaska, Hawaii, Nevada, and North Carolina) decreased their total amount of state expenditures and 46 states increased their total amount of state expenditures.

Table 3. Change in State General Fund Expenditures, FY2008-FY2010 ($ in millions)

State	State General Fund Expenditures, FY2008	State General Fund Expenditures, FY2010	Change in State General Fund Expenditures, FY2008 to FY2010
Alabama	$8,460	$6,847	-$1,613
Alaska	$5,090	$5,375	$285
Arizona	$10,368	$9,079	-$1,289
Arkansas	$4,274	$4,207	-$67
California	$102,986	$86,465	-$16,521
Colorado	$7,908	$7,326	-$582
Connecticut	$16,627	$17,251	$624
Delaware	$3,422	$3,077	-$345
Florida	$27,513	$21,195	-$6,318
Georgia	$17,934	$14,870	-$3,064
Hawaii	$5,407	$4,838	-$569
Idaho	$2,799	$2,349	-$450
Illinois	$22,140	$17,244	-$4,896
Indiana	$12,880	$12,915	$35
Iowa	$5,867	$5,302	-$565
Kansas	$6,102	$5,451	-$651
Kentucky	$9,334	$8,348	-$986
Louisiana	$10,372	$9,011	-$1,361
Maine	$3,084	$2,866	-$218
Maryland	$14,488	$13,428	-$1,060
Massachusetts	$28,934	$28,912	-$22
Michigan	$9,822	$8,110	-$1,712
Minnesota	$17,600	$15,567	-$2,033
Mississippi	$4,842	$4,597	-$245
Missouri	$8,084	$7,565	-$519
Montana	$1,901	$1,628	-$273
Nebraska	$3,247	$3,313	$66
Nevada	$4,031	$3,291	-$740
New Hampshire	$1,515	$1,401	-$114
New Jersey	$33,112	$29,862	-$3,250
New Mexico	$6,027	$5,468	-$559
New York	$53,385	$54,262	$877

State	State General Fund Expenditures, FY2008	State General Fund Expenditures, FY2010	Change in State General Fund Expenditures, FY2008 to FY2010
North Carolina	$20,376	$13,765	-$6,611
North Dakota	$1,204	$1,551	$347
Ohio	$25,722	$24,141	-$1,581
Oklahoma	$6,793	$6,036	-$757
Oregon	$6,601	$5,969	-$632
Pennsylvania	$26,969	$25,177	-$1,792
Rhode Island	$3,405	$2,887	-$518
South Carolina	$7,149	$5,275	-$1,874
South Dakota	$1,176	$1,129	-$47
Tennessee	$11,570	$10,671	-$899
Texas	$41,184	$44,156	$2,972
Utah	$5,784	$4,441	-$1,343
Vermont	$1,225	$1,109	-$116
Virginia	$15,099	$14,989	-$110
Washington	$14,616	$15,036	$420
West Virginia	$3,824	$3,779	-$45
Wisconsin	$13,527	$12,824	-$703
Wyoming	$3,132	$3,836	$704
Total	$678,911	$618,191	-$60,720

Source: CRS computations from National Association of State Budget Officers, FY2009 State Expenditure Report, Washington, DC, p. 6, *http://nasbo.org/LinkClick.aspx?fileticket=%2bPqnI4oZw2I%3d&tabid=79*.

Notes: FY2010 state general fund expenditures are estimated from state budget documents.

State General Fund Expenditures

In contrast to total state expenditures, which increased by nearly $145.9 billion from FY2008 to FY2010, state general fund expenditures decreased $60.7 billion from FY2008 ($678.9 billion) to FY2010 ($618.2 billion). As shown in Table 3, from FY2008 to FY2010, 41 states decreased their state general fund expenditures and 9 states (Alaska, Connecticut, Indiana,

Nebraska, New York, North Dakota, Texas, Washington, and Wyoming) increased their state general fund expenditures.

Table 4. Change in State Federal Funds Expenditures, FY2008-FY2010 ($ in millions)

State	State Federal Funds Expenditures, FY2008	State Federal Fund Expenditures, FY2010	Change in State Federal Fund Expenditures, FY2008 to FY2010
Alabama	$6,291	$10,181	$3,890
Alaska	$2,314	$3,178	$864
Arizona	$7,820	$10,655	$2,835
Arkansas	$4,806	$7,091	$2,285
California	$56,211	$95,398	$39,187
Colorado	$4,739	$8,920	$4,181
Connecticut	$2,117	$3,099	$982
Delaware	$1,113	$1,607	$494
Florida	$18,754	$22,744	$3,990
Georgia	$10,268	$13,066	$2,798
Hawaii	$1,760	$2,391	$631
Idaho	$2,005	$2,952	$947
Illinois	$11,073	$14,686	$3,613
Indiana	$7,818	$10,333	$2,515
Iowa	$4,565	$6,642	$2,077
Kansas	$3,522	$4,544	$1,022
Kentucky	$6,720	$10,477	$3,757
Louisiana	$12,883	$14,798	$1,915
Maine	$2,182	$3,151	$969
Maryland	$6,561	$9,795	$3,234
Massachusetts	$2,525	$5,722	$3,197
Michigan	$12,660	$19,238	$6,578
Minnesota	$6,264	$10,400	$4,136
Mississippi	$6,434	$8,832	$2,398
Missouri	$5,632	$8,743	$3,111
Montana	$1,646	$2,285	$639
Nebraska	$2,411	$2,973	$562
Nevada	$1,780	$2,705	$925
New Hampshire	$1,498	$2,073	$575

State	State Federal Funds Expenditures, FY2008	State Federal Fund Expenditures, FY2010	Change in State Federal Fund Expenditures, FY2008 to FY2010
New Jersey	$8,851	$14,045	$5,194
New Mexico	$4,506	$5,580	$1,074
New York	$34,680	$44,843	$10,163
North Carolina	$10,914	$10,492	-$422
North Dakota	$1,241	$1,767	$526
Ohio	$9,655	$13,029	$3,374
Oklahoma	$9,030	$10,899	$1,869
Oregon	$4,625	$8,275	$3,650
Pennsylvania	$18,037	$29,363	$11,326
Rhode Island	$1,939	$3,096	$1,157
South Carolina	$6,654	$10,117	$3,463
South Dakota	$1,182	$1,718	$536
Tennessee	$9,343	$12,903	$3,560
Texas	$25,023	$38,001	$12,978
Utah	$2,503	$3,672	$1,169
Vermont	$1,312	$1,845	$533
Virginia	$6,342	$9,327	$2,985
Washington	$6,678	$8,662	$1,984
West Virginia	$3,287	$4,418	$1,131
Wisconsin	$7,534	$11,531	$3,997
Wyoming	$476	$1,430	$954
Total	$388,184	$563,692	$175,508

Source: CRS computations from National Association of State Budget Officers, FY2009 State Expenditure Report, Washington, DC, p. 6, *http://nasbo .org/LinkClick.aspx?fileticket=%2bPqnI4oZw2I%3d&tabid=79*.

Notes: FY2010 state federal fund expenditures are estimated from state budget documents.

State Federal Funds Expenditures

As mentioned previously, most of the increase in total state expenditures from FY2008 to FY2010 came from the states' federal funds expenditures budgets. States spent $388.2 billion in federal assistance in FY2008, $457.0 billion in FY2009, and $563.7 billion in FY2010.

As shown in Table 4, state federal funds expenditures increased $175.5 billion from FY2008 to FY2010. One state (North Carolina) decreased its federal funds expenditures and 49 states increased their federal funds expenditures.

Table 5. Change in Other State Funds Expenditures, FY2008-FY2010 ($ in millions)

State	Other State Funds Expenditures, FY2008	Other State Funds Expenditures, FY2010	Change in Other State Funds Expenditures, FY2008 to FY2010
Alabama	$4,537	$7,024	$2,487
Alaska	$4,226	$1,193	-$3,033
Arizona	$6,405	$6,891	$486
Arkansas	$7,756	$8,862	$1,106
California	$26,674	$23,326	-$3,348
Colorado	$12,482	$12,757	$275
Connecticut	$3,494	$3,918	$424
Delaware	$3,811	$3,783	-$28
Florida	$14,916	$20,733	$5,817
Georgia	$8,773	$9,594	$821
Hawaii	$3,376	$3,045	-$331
Idaho	$1,097	$1,808	$711
Illinois	$11,047	$14,657	$3,610
Indiana	$3,380	$3,245	-$135
Iowa	$5,668	$6,143	$475
Kansas	$2,787	$4,178	$1,391
Kentucky	$6,941	$7,012	$71
Louisiana	$5,342	$5,177	-$165
Maine	$2,053	$2,159	$106
Maryland	$8,520	$9,058	$538
Massachusetts	$10,928	$16,889	$5,961
Michigan	$21,081	$18,183	-$2,898
Minnesota	$3,891	$4,792	$901
Mississippi	$4,029	$5,536	$1,507
Missouri	$7,165	$7,791	$626
Montana	$1,810	$2,136	$326
Nebraska	$3,053	$3,305	$252

State	Other State Funds Expenditures, FY2008	Other State Funds Expenditures, FY2010	Change in Other State Funds Expenditures, FY2008 to FY2010
Nevada	3,028	$1,702	-$1,326
New Hampshire	$1,680	$1,853	$173
New Jersey	$5,233	$3,411	-$1,822
New Mexico	$3,091	$2,711	-$380
New York	$26,122	$28,569	$2,447
North Carolina	$10,098	$7,046	-$3,052
North Dakota	$1,125	$1,370	$245
Ohio	$20,633	$19,827	-$806
Oklahoma	$4,803	$4,480	-$323
Oregon	$10,763	$13,203	$2,440
Pennsylvania	$12,952	$14,181	$1,229
Rhode Island	$1,589	$2,085	$496
South Carolina	$6,866	$7,175	$309
South Dakota	$842	$855	$13
Tennessee	$4,969	$5,291	$322
Texas	$12,634	$13,412	$778
Utah	$3,033	$3,555	$522
Vermont	$2,734	$2,796	$62
Virginia	$13,040	$15,001	$1,961
Washington	$8,617	$6,849	-$1,768
West Virginia	$11,422	$11,919	$497
Wisconsin	$15,028	$15,730	$702
Wyoming	$1,350	$2,391	$1,041
Total Change	$376,894	$398,607	$21,713

Source: CRS computations from National Association of State Budget Officers, FY2009 State Expenditure Report, Washington, DC, p. 6, *http://nasbo.org/LinkClick.aspx?fileticket=%2bPqnl4oZw2I%3d&tabid=79.*

Notes: FY2010 state other state fund expenditures are estimated from state budget documents.

Other State Funds Expenditures

States increased spending from their other state funds expenditures budgets from FY 2008 to FY20010. States spent $376.9 billion from their respective other state funds expenditure budgets in FY2008, $396.7 billion in FY2009, and $398.6 billion in FY2010.

As shown in Table 5, other state funds expenditures increased $21.7 billion from FY2008 to FY2010, with 14 states decreasing their other state funds expenditures and 36 states increasing their other state funds expenditures.

Table 6. Change in State Bonds Fund Expenditures, FY2008-FY2010 ($ in millions)

State	State Bonds Fund Expenditures, FY2008	State Bonds Fund Expenditures, FY2010	Change in State Bonds Fund Expenditures, FY2008 to FY2010
Alabama	$552	$406	-$146
Alaska	$26	$0	-$26
Arizona	$654	$886	$232
Arkansas	$63	$89	$26
California	$8,405	$12,653	$4,248
Colorado	$0	$0	$0
Connecticut	$2,032	$1,794	-$238
Delaware	$275	$253	-$22
Florida	$3,196	$1,833	-$1,363
Georgia	$1,519	$1,091	-$428
Hawaii	$617	$674	$57
Idaho	$31	$21	-$10
Illinois	$306	$839	$533
Indiana	$161	$169	$8
Iowa	$29	$459	$430
Kansas	$278	$324	$46
Kentucky	$0	$0	$0
Louisiana	$291	$626	$335
Maine	$108	$81	-$27
Maryland	$839	$1,128	$289
Massachusetts	$1,420	$1,887	$467
Michigan	$419	$192	-$227
Minnesota	$691	$743	$52
Mississippi	$234	$419	$185
Missouri	$551	$712	$161
Montana	$0	$0	$0
Nebraska	$0	$0	$0

State	State Bonds Fund Expenditures, FY2008	State Bonds Fund Expenditures, FY2010	Change in State Bonds Fund Expenditures, FY2008 to FY2010
Nevada	401	$177	-$224
New Hampshire	$114	$138	$24
New Jersey	$1,508	$1,657	$149
New Mexico	$583	$592	$9
New York	$1,869	$3,263	$1,394
North Carolina	$200	$489	$289
North Dakota	$27	$22	-$5
Ohio	$753	$643	-$110
Oklahoma	$104	$144	$40
Oregon	$185	$473	$288
Pennsylvania	$738	$1,655	$917
Rhode Island	$185	$94	-$91
South Carolina	$118	$0	-$118
South Dakota	$17	$67	$50
Tennessee	$151	$271	$120
Texas	$2,256	$2,298	$42
Utah	$3	$1,259	$1,256
Vermont	$37	$72	$35
Virginia	$849	$1,456	$607
Washington	$1,821	$1,996	$175
West Virginia	$177	$131	-$46
Wisconsin	$0	$0	$0
Wyoming	$0	$0	$0
Total Change	$34,793	$44,176	$9,383

Source: CRS computations from National Association of State Budget Officers, FY2009 State Expenditure Report, Washington, DC, p. 6, *http://nasbo.org/LinkClick.aspx?fileticket=%2bPqnI4oZw2I%3d&tabid=79*.

Notes: FY2010 state bonds fund expenditures are estimated from state budget documents.

State Bonds Expenditures

In FY2008, states spent $34.8 billion from their respective state bonds fund expenditure budgets. That amount increased to $36.4 billion in FY2009, and to $44.2 billion in FY2010. As shown in Table 6, six states (Colorado, Kentucky, Montana, Nebraska, Wisconsin, and Wyoming) had no state bonds fund expenditures in FY2008, FY2009, and FY2010.

Table 7. Change in State Capital Fund Expenditures, FY2008-FY2010 ($ in millions)

State	State Capital Fund Expenditures, FY2008	State Capital Fund Expenditures, FY2010	Change in State Capital Fund Expenditures, FY2008 to FY2010
Alabama	$1,256	$1,583	$327
Alaska	$2,606	$2,158	-$448
Arizona	$1,234	$1,181	-$53
Arkansas	$107	$216	$109
California	$5,210	$8,353	$3,143
Colorado	$1,798	$1,207	-$591
Connecticut	$2,032	$1,794	-$238
Delaware	$652	$662	$10
Florida	$12,671	$9,028	-$3,643
Georgia	$3,229	$2,717	-$512
Hawaii	$1,047	$1,178	$131
Idaho	$479	$717	$238
Illinois	$2,378	$4,192	$1,814
Indiana	$477	$447	-$30
Iowa	$598	$726	$128
Kansas	$782	$1,072	$290
Kentucky	$875	$1,069	$194
Louisiana	$1,710	$2,906	$1,196
Maine	$235	$298	$63
Maryland	$2,980	$3,429	$449
Massachusetts	$1,985	$2,615	$630
Michigan	$1,832	$2,771	$939
Minnesota	$1,503	$1,815	$312
Mississippi	$1,384	$1,366	-$18
Missouri	$223	$202	-$21
Montana	$0	$0	$0
Nebraska	$851	$922	$71
Nevada	1,240	$1,221	-$19
New Hampshire	$300	$296	-$4
New Jersey	$4,896	$4,547	-$349
New Mexico	$866	$396	-$470
New York	$6,131	$7,112	$981
North Carolina	$0	$0	$0

State	State Capital Fund Expenditures, FY2008	State Capital Fund Expenditures, FY2010	Change in State Capital Fund Expenditures, FY2008 to FY2010
North Dakota	$403	$530	$127
Ohio	$3,004	$4,632	$1,628
Oklahoma	$1,572	$1,401	-$171
Oregon	$310	$647	$337
Pennsylvania	$738	$1,655	$917
Rhode Island	$429	$597	$168
South Carolina	$436	$0	-$436
South Dakota	$74	$101	$27
Tennessee	$1,609	$1,614	$5
Texas	$148	$279	$131
Utah	$1,735	$2,230	$495
Vermont	$225	$337	$112
Virginia	$1,192	$1,381	$189
Washington	$3,576	$3,477	-$99
West Virginia	$1,091	$1,355	$264
Wisconsin	$0	$0	$0
Wyoming	$239	$353	$114
Total Change	$80,347	$88,785	$8,437

Source: CRS computations from National Association of State Budget Officers, FY2009 State Expenditure Report, Washington, DC, p. 6, *http://nasbo.org /LinkClick.aspx?fileticket=%2bPqnI4oZw2I%3d&tabid=79*.

Notes: FY2010 state capital fund expenditures are estimated from state budget documents.

The remaining 44 states collectively increased their state bond fund expenditures by almost $9.4 billion from FY2008 to FY2010, with 15 states decreasing their state bonds fund expenditures and 29 states increasing their state bonds fund expenditures.

State Capital Expenditures

The total state expenditures amounts presented in Table 2 included state capital expenditures. As mentioned previously, state capital expenditures totaled $80.3 billion in FY2008, $84.2 billion in FY2009, and an estimated $88.8 billion in FY2010.[33] As shown in Table 7, three states (Montana, North

Carolina, and Wisconsin) had no state capital expenditures in FY2008, FY2009, and FY2010. The remaining 47 states collectively increased their state capital fund expenditures by more than $8.4 billion from FY2008 to FY2010, with 16 states decreasing their state capital fund expenditures and 31 states increasing their state capital fund expenditures.

FEDERAL ASSISTANCE AND STATE FISCAL STRESS

As the data in the preceding tables indicate, from FY2008 to FY 2010, states became increasingly reliant on federal assistance. For example, as mentioned previously, expenditures from the states' federal funds budgets increased by $175.5 billion from FY2008 to FY2010, compared to an increase of $21.7 billion from the states' other state funds budgets, an increase of $9.4 billion from the states' bonds budgets, and a decrease of $60.7 billion from the states' general fund budgets.

Table 8. Total Amount of State Federal Assistance and Federal Assistance as a Share of Total State Expenditures (Capital Inclusive), FY2000-FY2010 ($ in millions)

FY	Total Amount of State Federal Assistance	% Share of Total State Expenditures
2000	$241,317	26.0%
2001	$260,567	25.8%
2002	$295,752	26.9%
2003	$325,102	28.7%
2004	$343,561	29.5%
2005	$365,787	28.9%
2006	$368,668	27.8%
2007	$379,271	26.5%
2008	$388,184	26.3%
2009	$456,968	29.5%
2010 est.	$563,692	34.7%

Source: National Association of State Budget Officers, various FY State Expenditure Reports, Washington, DC, from FY2000-FY2009, all pp. 4, 8, *http://nasbo.org* /Publications/StateExpenditureReport/StateExpenditureReportArchives/tabid/107/ Default.aspx.

Also, as shown on Table 8, the total amount of state federal assistance has increased each fiscal year since FY2000, reaching 34.7% of total state expenditures in FY2010. State budget officials anticipate that this upward trend in state federal assistance will end over the next several years as ARRA-related funding is exhausted and federal policymakers scrutinize the federal budget in an effort to address the federal budget deficit. President Obama's FY2012 budget request supports this view, projecting a decline in federal grant-in-aid funding for state and local governments combined from $625.2 billion in FY2011 to $584.3 billion in FY2012 and $567.5 billion in FY2013.[34]

Consequences for State Policymakers

The states' increased reliance on federal assistance has consequences for both state and federal policymakers. For example, in the past, state political leaders have generally welcomed increased levels of federal assistance while, at the same time, requesting that states be provided maximum feasible flexibility in the use of the grant funds. For example, the National Governors Association (NGA) adopted a permanent policy statement on state-federal relations in 1993, which has been subsequently reaffirmed on several occasions. NGA recommends, among other actions, that the federal government avoid preemption of state laws and policies, preserve state standards, not interfere with state revenue systems, avoid unfunded federal mandates, and provide maximum state flexibility in the use of the federal funds without specific set-asides.[35]

With the notable exception of a few governors who objected to federal conditions attached to ARRA-funded, optional unemployment insurance modernization incentive payments, state policymakers have generally welcomed the recent increase in state federal assistance as a means to help them cope with reductions in state revenues. It is possible, however, that this increased reliance on state federal assistance might also further limit the states' ability to determine their own policy choices. For example, the need to comply with federal conditions attached to the increased level of federal funds may limit the states' ability to design programs in a way that they believe best meets their needs, which could lead to the federal government substituting its policy preferences for the state's policy preferences. Also, given the current relatively low rate of growth for state tax revenue, the states' increased reliance on federal assistance could limit the states' ability to finance non-federal programs because many federal grants, including Medicaid, have mandatory state matching requirements.

It could also be argued that the states' increased reliance on federal assistance could induce a moral hazard issue by encouraging states to expect similar increases in federal assistance during future economic slowdowns. The concern is that by providing states additional federal assistance the states' "incentives to properly manage risks," by taking such actions as fully funding their "rainy day" reserve funds or making other policy choices to restrain state budget growth during good economic times, could be weakened.[36]

Consequences for Congress

The states' increased reliance on federal assistance could make it more difficult for Congress to make quick and deep reductions in state federal assistance because such actions could lead state governments to take actions, such as laying off public employees, cutting back on state service levels, or increasing state taxes and fees, that could have an adverse affect on the national economic recovery. It could also be argued that many states would have to take such actions because they presently lack the own-source revenue necessary to absorb a significant reduction in state federal assistance.

The counter-argument is that the consequences of reducing state federal assistance to pre-recession levels may force some state governments to make difficult policy choices, but, given the federal government's budget deficit and debt, federal policymakers face similar difficult choices. In addition, it could be argued that the states' increased reliance on federal assistance has created conditions in which state service and benefits levels have become artificially "elevated" to levels that, in the absence of additional federal assistance, would not have been enacted in the first place. As will be discussed in the next section, this last argument involves value judgments concerning the appropriate size and scope of state government.

Variations in State Fiscal Stress

As mentioned previously, although state economic downturns generally occur around the same time as national recessions, the states' responses to national recessions "vary in magnitude, duration, and timing and do not necessarily coincide with dates identified for national recessions."[37] The variation in the states' economic responses to the most recent recession helps to explain the variation found in the states' change in state general fund expenditures from FY2008 to FY2010, with some states increasing their state general fund expenditures and others cutting them.

Consequences for Congress

GAO has recommended that Congress take variations in state fiscal stress into consideration when deciding whether, when, and how to provide federal assistance to state and local governments during and immediately after national economic downturns.[38] Specifically, GAO found that the federal government has provided fiscal assistance to state and local governments in response to three of the six national recessions since 1974, and, after examining the efficacy of those efforts in ameliorating state fiscal stress and enhancing national economic growth, recommended that Congress consider the following when developing a policy strategy to address state and local government fiscal stress during and following national recessions:

- Timing/triggering mechanisms—federal policy strategies specifically intended to stabilize state and local governments' budgets may have to be timed differently than those designed to stimulate the national economy, because state budget difficulties often persist beyond the end of a recession.
- Targeting—if federal fiscal assistance to state and local governments is targeted based on the magnitude of the recession's effect on each state's economy, this approach can facilitate economic recovery and moderate fiscal distress at the state and local level.
- Temporary—while a federal fiscal stimulus strategy can increase economic growth in the short run, such efforts can contribute to the federal budget deficit if allowed to run too long after entering a period of strong recovery.
- Consistency—the design of federal fiscal assistance occurs in tandem with consideration of the impact these strategies can have on other federal policy objectives. For example, a standby federal fiscal assistance policy could induce moral hazard by encouraging state or local governments to expect similar federal action in future crises, thereby weakening their incentives to properly manage risks. Another consideration is the policy objective of maintaining accountability while promoting flexibility in state spending. Past studies have shown

> that unrestricted federal funds are fungible and can be substituted for state funds, and the uses of such funds can be difficult or impossible to track.[39]

GAO provided Congress a list of recommended economic indicators that could be used to serve as triggering mechanisms to either time or target state federal assistance to respond to the effects of a particular recession, including, among others: employment and unemployment data, hourly earnings, personal income, wages and salaries, and weekly hours worked.[40] GAO excluded indicators of state fiscal stress, such as declines in state tax receipts or state budget gaps, "because they are dependent on state government's policy choices and because state definitions and measurement techniques vary for calculations such as budget gaps."[41]

Benchmarks for Measuring Variation in State Fiscal Stress

Although GAO chose not to measure variations in state fiscal assistance, one measure of state fiscal stress that is often used is the difference between the state's current and previous year's general fund budget expenditures. It could be argued that if the state is facing a need to reduce its general fund expenditures from the previous year's level, either in real (inflation adjusted) dollars or in current (nominal) dollars, it is experiencing fiscal stress. Generally speaking, after taking into account factors such as state population differences or differences in the size of the states' general fund budgets, as the amount needed to reduce the state's general fund expenditures increases (typically referred to as the state's budget gap), the state's fiscal stress also increases.

Issues with Using State General Fund Expenditures as a Benchmark

The difference between each state's current and previous year general fund budget expenditures is relatively easy to compute and is often used as an indication of state fiscal stress by various organizations. However, as GAO has noted, there is little guidance available to determine if the state's general fund expenditures for the current, or for the previous year, are "appropriate" baselines to use for measuring state fiscal stress. For example, depending on one's personal values concerning the appropriate size and scope of state government, it could be argued that state expenditures are too high or too low. Also, as mentioned previously, in the absence of an agreement concerning which baselines to use in measuring state fiscal stress, it could be argued that the states' current fiscal stress has as much to do with their previous budgetary decisions (or non-decisions) than with the national economic slowdown's adverse affect on state revenue growth. This is an important issue for federal policymakers because if state fiscal stress is viewed as being largely a result of state policy decisions, it is likely that there will be less support for federal action to ease that fiscal stress than would be the case otherwise.

Measuring the Relative Size of State Governments

The data presented in the Table 9 is provided to help inform congressional debate concerning the extent to which the states' varying levels of fiscal stress is due to changing economic conditions or to state policy choices. The data provide a framework for measuring differences in the size of state governments relative to each other, rather than to a preconceived "ideal" state budget that would, by necessity, be based largely on personal value judgments concerning the appropriate size and scope of state government. This information may prove useful as a reference when debating the role of state policy choice in state fiscal stress.

As shown in the table, total state expenditures, both per capita and as a percentage of state GDP, vary.[42]

As shown in Table 9, in FY2010, total state expenditures ranged from $3,769 million in South Dakota to $217,842 million in California. The national average for total state expenditures was $34,493 million, with 37 states having total state expenditures below the national average and 13 states having total state expenditures above the national average.

In FY2010, total state expenditures on a per capita basis varied from $2,907 in Nevada to $13,508 in Alaska. The national average for total state expenditures on a per capita basis was $5,255, with 23 states having total state expenditures on a per capita below the national average and 27 states having total state expenditures on a per capita basis above the national average.

In FY2009 (the latest data available), state gross domestic product and total state expenditures as a percentage of state gross domestic product varied from state-to-state. State gross domestic product ranged from $25,121 million in Vermont to $1,884,452 million in California. The national average for state gross domestic product was $278,569 million, with 37 states having state gross domestic product below the national average and 13 states having state gross domestic product above the national average.

Table 9. Total State Expenditures, Per Capita FY2010 and Percentage of State GDP FY2009

State	Total State Expenditures FY2010 ($ in millions)	Total State Expenditures FY2010, Per Capita	State GDP FY2009 ($ in millions)	Total State Expenditures FY2009, % of State GDP
Alabama	$24,458	$5,092	$168,368	11.74%
Alaska	$9,746	$13,508	$46,664	28.98%
Arizona	$27,511	$4,290	$254,099	10.66%
Arkansas	$20,249	$6,920	$100,753	18.06%
California	$217,842	$5,834	$1,884,452	10.37%
Colorado	$29,003	$5,749	$250,930	11.48%
Connecticut	$26,062	$7,277	$220,372	11.71%
Delaware	$8,720	$9,679	$59,328	14.73%
Florida	$66,505	$3,519	$729,485	8.32%
Georgia	$38,621	$3,970	$393,380	9.91%
Hawaii	$10,948	$8,010	$65,680	18.00%
Idaho	$7,130	$4,531	$53,488	11.80%
Illinois	$47,426	$3,687	$621,101	7.48%
Indiana	$26,662	$4,101	$257,463	9.99%
Iowa	$18,546	$6,073	$136,341	12.82%
Kansas	$14,497	$5,062	$123,449	11.31%
Kentucky	$25,837	$5,939	$154,558	15.57%
Louisiana	$29,612	$6,502	$208,392	12.31%
Maine	$8,257	$6,194	$50,645	15.98%
Maryland	$33,409	$5,770	$283,801	11.20%
Massachusetts	$53,410	$8,142	$362,413	13.52%
Michigan	$45,723	$4,613	$361,126	12.67%
Minnesota	$31,502	$5,927	$257,583	11.61%
Mississippi	$19,384	$6,509	$95,055	17.18%
Missouri	$24,811	$4,127	$236,749	9.75%
Montana	$6,049	$6,083	$35,609	15.52%
Nebraska	$9,591	$5,236	$84,575	10.81%
Nevada	$7,875	$2,907	$125,115	7.22%
New Hampshire	$5,465	$4,136	$58,937	8.45%
New Jersey	$48,975	$5,561	$478,391	9.76%
New Mexico	$14,351	$6,942	$74,388	20.84%
New York	$130,937	$6,742	$1,085,131	11.20%
North Carolina	$31,792	$3,324	$398,902	10.80%

State	Total State Expenditures FY2010 ($ in millions)	Total State Expenditures FY2010, Per Capita	State GDP FY2009 ($ in millions)	Total State Expenditures FY2009, % of State GDP
North Dakota	$4,710	$6,968	$31,626	12.46%
Ohio	$57,640	$4,982	$466,021	12.40%
Oklahoma	$21,559	$5,726	$154,296	13.89%
Oregon	$27,920	$7,255	$165,176	14.85%
Pennsylvania	$70,376	$5,526	$547,865	11.43%
Rhode Island	$8,162	$7,735	$47,598	14.92%
South Carolina	$22,567	$4,857	$157,990	13.34%
South Dakota	$3,769	$4,598	$38,774	9.15%
Tennessee	$29,136	$4,570	$241,907	12.04%
Texas	$97,867	$3,873	$1,141,287	7.88%
Utah	$12,927	$4,665	$112,671	10.47%
Vermont	$5,822	$9,236	$25,121	22.36%
Virginia	$40,773	$5,073	$406,305	9.85%
Washington	$32,543	$4,819	$336,325	10.02%
West Virginia	$20,247	$10,887	$62,258	32.84%
Wisconsin	$40,085	$7,035	$239,061	16.08%
Wyoming	$7,657	$13,474	$37,462	20.42%
Total	$1,624,666	NA	$13,928,466	NA
National Average	$32,493	$5,255	$278,569	11.11%

Source: CRS computations from U.S. Bureau of the Census," Apportionment Population and Number of Representatives, by State: 2010 Census," Washington, DC, December 21, 2010, http://www.thegreenpapers.com/Census10/; U.S. Department of Commerce, Bureau of Economic Analysis, "Gross Domestic Product By State," Washington, DC, February 23, 2011, *http://www.bea .gov/regional/gsp/*; and National Association of State Budget Officers, FY2009 State Expenditure Report, Washington, DC, p. 6, *http://nasbo.org/LinkClick .aspx?fileticket=%2bPqnl4oZw2I%3d&tabid=79;*

Notes: FY2010 total state expenditures are estimated from state budget documents. The national median for total state expenditures FY2010, per capita, was $9,283. The national median for total state expenditures FY2009, % of state GDP, was 16.08%.

In FY2009, total state expenditures as a percentage of state gross domestic product ranged from 7.22% in Nevada to 32.84% in West Virginia. The national average for total state expenditures as a percentage of state gross domestic product was 11.11%, with 17 states having total state expenditures as a percentage of state gross domestic product below the national average and 33 states having total state expenditures as a percentage of state gross domestic product above the national average.

CONCLUSION

State policymakers throughout the nation will face at least four significant fiscal challenges in the coming years. First, state budget officials expect relatively low levels of tax revenue growth. If these state revenue estimates prove to be accurate, unless there is growth in other state revenue sources, many states are going to face funding gaps in their general fund budgets for several more years which, given state balanced operating budget requirements, will need to be addressed.[43] Second, ARRA funding, the primary source of state revenue relief over the past two years, is expiring. Third, state federal assistance outside of ARRA is expected to decline, and federal grants to state and local governments are included in federal domestic discretionary spending, an area of the federal budget expected to receive much attention over the next several years by federal policymakers as they seek ways to address the federal deficit and debt. Fourth, projected state costs for Medicaid, state employee pension and retirement health care obligations, and delayed infrastructure projects are also expected to provide continuing budgetary challenges for states.

Given these fiscal challenges, it is likely that states will continue to look to the federal government for financial assistance. Federal assistance could be provided in several ways, for example (1) granting of waivers of federal grant program requirements, (2) temporary or permanent relief from federal grant matching requirements, (3) relaxation or elimination of state program-related maintenance of effort requirements that are often attached to federal grant programs, and (4) providing additional direct federal assistance.

GAO has recommended that Congress consider variations in state fiscal stress when deciding whether, when, and how to provide federal assistance to state and local governments during and immediately after national economic downturns. As mentioned previously, GAO also provided a list of economic indicators, such as employment and unemployment data, hourly earnings, personal income, wages and salaries, and weekly hours worked, that could be used as triggers for providing states federal assistance.[44] GAO excluded indicators of state fiscal stress, such as declines in state tax receipts or state budget gaps, "because they are dependent on state government's policy choices and because state definitions and measurement techniques vary for calculations such as budget gaps."[45]

Disagreements over the appropriate size of state government has always been an issue in discussions of the role of federal assistance in state budgeting. The data presented in Table 9 suggest that state governments, both in terms of total state expenditures on a per capita basis and as a percentage of state GDP, vary in size. Some argue against providing additional federal assistance to states because, in their view, the states' current level of fiscal stress, especially in states with a relatively high level of state expenditures, could have been ameliorated if the states had been more prudent with their fiscal choices prior to the recent recession. Others suggest that the federal government's fiscal challenges have reached a point in which providing additional federal assistance to states is out of the question. Still others assert that if the federal government does not continue to provide the states additional assistance that the states will take actions that will have an adverse affect on the national economic recovery. Some also contend that the recent increase in federal assistance to states is approaching levels that may lead to a fundamental change in the nature of American federalism. They are concerned that the need to match federal grant money and the increased reliance on federal assistance to provide services could displace state priorities with federal priorities. The data and analysis in this report provide a framework for assisting Congress as it considers these various viewpoints concerning whether, when, and how to provide federal assistance to state and local governments during times of state fiscal stress.

End Notes

[1] The state expenditure data presented in this report are drawn from the National Association of State Budget Officers' (NASBO) annual State Expenditure Reports. The data are self-reported by the states. In 2010, the Government Accountability Office (GAO) assessed the reliability of NASBO expenditure data for a report on state and local government use of funding provided by P.L. 111-5, the American Recovery and Reinvestment Act of 2009. GAO reviewed existing documentation related to the NASBO data sources and interviewed knowledgeable agency officials about the data. GAO determined that "the data are sufficiently reliable for the purposes of this report." See U.S. Government Accountability Office, *Recovery Act: Opportunities to Improve Management and Strengthen Accountability over States' and Localities' Use of Funds*, GAO-10-999, September 20, 2010, p. 205, http://www.gao.gov/new.items/d10999.pdf. GAO has also examined the reliability of NASBO's semi-annual Fiscal Survey of States reports and found them to be reliable. See U.S. Government Accountability Office, *State and Local Governments: Knowledge of Past*

Recessions Can Inform Future Federal Assistance, GAO-11-401, March 31, 2011, pp. 2, 52, http://www.gao.gov/new.items/d11401.pdf. The Bureau of the Census also surveys state and local governments concerning their revenues and expenditures. NASBO data was used in this report because it includes estimates for FY2010.

[2] National Association of State Budget Officers, *Budget Processes in the States*, Washington, DC, Summer 2008, p. 5, *http://nasbo.org/LinkClick.aspx?fileticket=AaAKTnjgucg%3d* &tabid=38.

[3] Ibid.

[4] Ibid., pp. 3, 20. For further information and analysis of state revenue estimates see Susan K. Urahn and Thomas Gais, "States' Revenue Estimating: Cracks in the Crystal Ball," The Nelson Rockefeller Institute of Government and the Pew Center on the States, Washington, DC, http://www.pewcenteronthestates.org/uploadedFiles/ States_Revenue_Estimating _final.pdf.

[5] National Association of State Budget Officers, *Budget Processes in the States*, Washington, DC, Summer 2008, pp. 3, 20, *http://nasbo.org/LinkClick.aspx?fileticket*=AaAKTnjgucg %3d&tabid=38.Ibid.

[6] Ibid., p. 40; and National Conference of State Legislatures, "NCSL Fiscal Brief: State Balanced Budget Provisions," Washington, DC, October 2010, pp. 4, 5, *http://www.ncsl.org* /documents/fiscal/ StateBalancedBudgetProvisions2010.pdf.

[7] National Association of State Budget Officers, *Budget Processes in the States*, Washington, DC, Summer 2008, pp. 29, 40, *http://nasbo.org/LinkClick.aspx?fileticket*=AaAKTnjgucg %3d&tabid=38.

[8] Ibid., p. 29, 38.

[9] Ibid., p. 43.

[10] U.S. Census Bureau, *State Government Finances Summary: 2009*, Government Division Briefs, Washington, DC, January 2011, p. 2, *http://www2.census.gov/govs/state*/09 statesummaryreport.pdf. For further analysis of state debt issues see CRS Report R41735, *State and Local Government Debt: An Analysis*, by Steven Maguire.

[11] National Association of State Budget Officers, *The Fiscal Survey of States*, Washington, DC, Fall 2010, pp. vii, viii, *http://nasbo.org/LinkClick.aspx?fileticket=C6q1M3kxaEY* %3d&tabid=83.

[12] Ibid., p. vii.

[13] Ibid.

[14] Ibid., pp. vii, viii; and National Association of State Budget Officers, "Preliminary Summary: NGA/NASBO Fall 2010 Fiscal Survey of States," Washington, DC, November 19, 2010, http://www.nasbo.org/LinkClick.aspx?fileticket= wJKroFj6QDA%3d&tabid=38.

[15] National Association of State Budget Officers, *The Fiscal Survey of States*, Washington, DC, Fall 2010, pp. vii, viii, *http://nasbo.org/LinkClick.aspx?fileticket=C6q1M3kxaEY* %3d&tabid=83. The National Association of State Budget Officers reports that just over $43.2 billion in ARRA funding for the states will be available in FY2011. The Government Accountability Office reports that ARRA provided state and local governments about $282 billion in federal assistance. See U.S. Government Accountability Office, *State and Local Governments: Knowledge of Past Recessions Can Inform Future Federal Fiscal Assistance*, GAO-11-401, March 31, 2010, p. 1, http://www.gao.gov/new.items/d11401.pdf.

[16] National Governors Association, "NGA, NASBO Say Fiscal 2011 Will Be Another Difficult Year for States," Washington, DC, December 1, 2010, http://www.nga.org/portal/site/nga/ menuitem.6c9a8a9ebc6ae07eee28aca9501010a0/?vgnextoid=10be80bc9c89c210VgnVCM 1000005e00100aRCRD&vg nextchannel=759b8f2005361010VgnVCM1000001a01010aRCRD; National Association of State Budget Officers, "Facts You Should Know: State and Local Bankruptcy, Municipal Bonds, State and Local Pensions," Washington, DC, 2010, *http://www.nasbo.org* /LinkClick.aspx?fileticket=TPVfxV3%2fn10%3d&tabid=38; Dean Baker, "The Origins and Severity of the Public Pension Crisis," Center for Economic and Policy Research,

Washington, DC, February 2011, http://www.cepr.net/documents/publications/pensions-2011-02.pdf; The Pew Center on the States, "The Trillion Dollar Gap: Underfunded State Retirement Systems and the Road Ahead," Washington, DC, February 2010, http://downloads.pewcenteronthestates.org/The_Trillion_Dollar_Gap_final.pdf; and CRS Report R41736, *State and Local Pension Plans and Fiscal Distress: A Legal Overview*, by Jennifer Staman.

[17] Benjamin S. Bernanke, Chairman, Board of Governors of the Federal Reserve Board, "Challenges for State and Local Governments," presentation at the 2011 Annual Awards Dinner of the Citizens Budget Commission, New York, March 2, 2011, http://www.federalreserve.gov/newsevents/speech/bernanke20110302a.htm.

[18] National Association of State Budget Officers, *Budget Processes in the States*, Washington, DC, Summer 2008, pp. 40, 43, *http://nasbo.org/LinkClick.aspx?fileticket*=AaAKTnjgucg%3d&tabid=38.

[19] Ibid., p. 107; and National Association of State Budget Officers, *State Expenditure Report: Fiscal Year 2009*, Washington, DC, December 2010, p. 4, *http://www.nasbo.org/LinkClick*.aspx?fileticket=w7RqO74lIEw%3d&tabid= 79.

[20] National Association of State Budget Officers, *Budget Processes in the States*, Washington, DC, Summer 2008, pp. 67-69, *http://nasbo.org/LinkClick.aspx?fileticket*=AaAKTnjgucg%3d&tabid=38.

[21] National Association of State Budget Officers, *The Fiscal Survey of States*, Washington, DC, Fall 2010, p. 49, http://nasbo.org/LinkClick.aspx?fileticket=C6q1M3kxaEY%3d&tabid=83. The procedures used to expend these funds also vary from state-to-state, with some states requiring a majority vote of the state legislature and others requiring a super majority vote to access the funds. See National Association of State Budget Officers, *Budget Processes in the States*, Washington, DC, Summer 2008, p. 50, *http://nasbo.org/LinkClick*.aspx?fileticket=AaAKTnjgucg%3d&tabid= 38.

[22] National Association of State Budget Officers, *The Fiscal Survey of States*, Washington, DC, Fall 2010, p. 50, http://nasbo.org/LinkClick.aspx?fileticket=C6q1M3kxaEY%3d&tabid=83.

[23] Ibid., p. 49.

[24] Ibid., p. 50.

[25] Ibid., p. 107; and National Association of State Budget Officers, *State Expenditure Report: Fiscal Year 2009*, Washington, DC, December 2010, p. 80, *http://www.nasbo.org/LinkClick*.aspx?fileticket=w7RqO74lIEw%3d&tabid= 79.

[26] National Association of State Budget Officers, *State Expenditure Report: Fiscal Year 2009*, Washington, DC, December 2010, p. 80, *http://www.nasbo.org/LinkClick.aspx?fileticket*=w7RqO74lIEw%3d&tabid=79.

[27] For further analysis of Build America Bonds, Recovery Zone Economic Development Bonds, and School Construction Bonds, see CRS Report R40523, *Tax Credit Bonds: Overview and Analysis*, by Steven Maguire.

[28] National Association of State Budget Officers, *State Expenditure Report: Fiscal Year 2009*, Washington, DC, December 2010, p. 81, *http://www.nasbo.org/LinkClick.aspx*?fileticket=w7RqO74lIEw%3d&tabid=79.

[29] H.Res. 38, Reducing non-security spending to fiscal year 2008 levels or less, was passed by the House, by a vote of 256-165, on January 25, 2011.

[30] National Association of State Budget Officers, *State Expenditure Report: Fiscal Year 2009*, Washington, DC, December 2010, p. 2, *http://www.nasbo.org/LinkClick.aspx?fileticket*=w7RqO74lIEw%3d&tabid=79.

[31] U.S. Government Accountability Office, *State and Local Governments: Knowledge of Past Recessions Can Inform Future Federal Fiscal Assistance*, GAO-11-401, March 31, 2010, p. 15, http://www.gao.gov/new.items/d11401.pdf.

[32] Ibid., p. 6.

[33] National Association of State Budget Officers, *State Expenditure Report: Fiscal Year 2009*, Washington, DC, December 2010, p. 80, *http://www.nasbo.org/LinkClick.aspx*?fileticket =w7RqO74lIEw%3d&tabid=79.

[34] U.S. Office of Management and Budget, *Budget of the United States Government, Fiscal Year 2012, Historical Tables*, Washington, DC, 2010, p. 251, *http://www.whitehouse.gov/sites* /default/files/omb/budget/fy2012/ assets/hist.pdf.

[35] National Governors Association, "Policy Statement: Permanent Policy. Principles for State-Federal Relations," Washington, DC, *http://www.nga.org/portal/site/nga/menuitem* .8358ec82f5b198d18a278110501010a0/?vgnextoid= 57c5e790fa435010VgnVCM1000001a01010aRCRD.

[36] U.S. Government Accountability Office, *State and Local Governments: Knowledge of Past Recessions Can Inform Future Federal Fiscal Assistance*, GAO-11-401, March 31, 2010, p. 30, http://www.gao.gov/new.items/d11401.pdf.

[37] Ibid., p. 3.

[38] Ibid., p. 28.

[39] Ibid., p. 30.

[40] Ibid., p. 32.

[41] Ibid.

[42] Another factor that could be used to compare total state expenditures is the extent to which the state relies on local governments to provide services. It could be argued that some states look "bigger" than others because they carry greater responsibility for providing services than their local governments when compared to other states. Unfortunately, data on local government finance are typically delayed for at least two years. For example, at the time of this writing, the latest available data at the Bureau of the Census for both state and local government expenditures is for FY2008. That data indicates that in FY2008 the state share of total state and local government expenditures varied among the states, ranging from 41.6% in Nebraska to 78.9% in Hawaii. The states' average share of state and local government expenditures was 52.3%, with 11 states below the national average and 39 states above the national average. CRS calculations from U.S. Bureau of the Census, "State and Local Government Finance: 2008 State and Local Government," Washington, DC, http://www.census.gov/govs/estimate/.

[43] For further information and analysis of state revenue estimates see Susan K. Urahn and Thomas Gais, "States' Revenue Estimating: Cracks in the Crystal Ball," The Nelson Rockefeller Institute of Government and the Pew Center on the States, Washington, DC, http://www.pewcenteronthestates.org/uploadedFiles/ States_Revenue_Estimating_final.pdf.

[44] Ibid., p. 32.

[45] Ibid.

In: The Fiscal Strains on State Governments
Editor: Arthur Horváth
ISBN: 978-1-62100-046-4

Chapter 2

STATE AND LOCAL GOVERNMENT DEBT: AN ANALYSIS

Steven Maguire

SUMMARY

The financial consequences of the recession that spanned from December 2007 through June 2009 have increased congressional interest in the financial health of state and local governments. State and local tax revenues declined, expenditures climbed, and debt increased. Even though tax revenue has begun to rebound, expenditures for unemployment benefits and other social programs remain elevated. Also, federal aid to states, which had increased as part of the American Recovery and Reinvestment Act, has begun to recede. Federal outlays for grants in aid to state and local governments rose from \$538 billion in FY2009 to \$608.4 billion in FY2010 and are estimated to be \$625.2 billion in FY2011. The FY2012 budget provides \$584.3 billion in outlays for aid to state and local governments in 2012.

In response to these state and local government fiscal headwinds, several hearings have been held early in the 112th Congress to examine the health of state and local government finances and the potential effects on the economic recovery. The hearings focused on a range of issues important to state and local governments as well as federal policy makers. The role of state and local government debt was one of these issues. The federal government has a significant stake in this debt market, as the tax expenditure for tax-exempt bonds issued by state and local governments was recently estimated to be $161.6 billion over the 2010 to 2014 budget window.

This report first provides a broad overview of state and local government finances and how these governments incorporate borrowing into their budgets. The second section reports data on state and local government debt and how that debt has changed over time. This section includes a comparative analysis of these debt parameters for each state. The third section discusses different economic perspectives on the use of debt by governments and if governments are intrinsically biased toward borrowing more than is considered economically optimal. The discussion provides background for Congress as it deliberates potential changes in the oversight of the primary and secondary markets for state and local government debt.

Issues related to state and local government finances, such as government pensions and health benefits, are also addressed.

STATE AND LOCAL GOVERNMENT FINANCES

The fiscal health of many states has been severely strained by the prolonged economic slowdown following the recent recession, even after the official end of the recession in June 2009. State and local tax revenues have declined, expenditures for social insurance programs have increased, and federal assistance has begun to recede as federal aid related to the American Recovery and Reinvestment Act (ARRA) expires. Further, state and local governments are required to balance current operating budgets either annually or biannually. State and local governments have used a combination of rainy day fund withdrawals, tax increases, spending reductions, and in some instances, borrowing to meet these balanced budget requirements.[1]

Congress has become increasingly concerned that state financial difficulties may lead states to take actions that could have an adverse impact on the economic recovery and that they may need additional federal government assistance. Part of this concern has focused on debt issued by state and local governments. This report will describe state and local government debt and analyze how debt is incorporated into state and local budgets. The report will also analyze the role the federal government has in state and local government debt structure.

Other issues of interest to Congress include bond default risk (or more generally, state bankruptcy) and public pension underfunding. Bond default risk and underfunding public pensions are both integral parts of state and local finance, though somewhat beyond the scope of this report. Clearly, during economic downturns, the risk of bond default rises. In particular, those bonds secured by specific revenue streams and not the general obligation of the issuing jurisdiction are at greatest risk. Even so, municipal default has been relatively rare, only 54 defaults from 1970 to 2009, and has yet to become a significant issue in municipal finance.[2] As for public pensions, debt is rarely used to finance future obligations and is generally discouraged by public finance professionals. Nonetheless, some states have used debt to fund pensions.[3]

State and Local Government Debt

As noted earlier, the level of state and local government debt and purported growth of this debt during the recession has generated significant congressional interest.[4] Some observers have suggested that the pressure to provide additional federal assistance has increased as states are purportedly relying more on debt to finance operations. For example, H.R. 344, the Fiscal Responsibility Effective Enforcement Act, would prohibit the Federal Reserve Board (the Fed) from buying short-term municipal securities, thus reducing the probability that the Fed would be asked to “bail-out” state and local governments. Congress has also held several hearings on policies addressing the fiscal health of state and local governments.[5] This section will describe the type of state and local government debt analyzed here and who holds this debt.

Operating Budget and Capital Budget

In contrast to the federal government, most state and local governments maintain two budgets, an operating budget and a capital budget. The operating budget funds current expenditures such as employee salaries, payment for services, and interest payments on debt. Current revenues, such as taxes, fees, user charges, and intergovernmental aid, finance these expenditures. When observers refer to state and local government budget deficits, they are almost always referring to the operating budget.

The timing of state and local revenue collection, however, typically does not match spending. Thus, most governments issue short-term debt to finance current spending then use future revenue to repay this debt. These notes are called revenue anticipation notes or tax anticipation notes. It is important to note that almost every state and local government is required to maintain a balanced operating budget from fiscal year to fiscal year, so only in rare circumstances is short-term debt carried over into the next fiscal year.[6]

The capital budget is typically used to finance infrastructure (or public capital) investment. The capital budget looks forward as far as 10 years for some states.[7] The role of debt differs in the operating and capital budgets. Long-term debt is almost always intended for capital projects and as such is included in the capital budget. However, the interest expense on debt issued for the capital budget is included in the operating budget.

No uniform definition of a "capital" expenditure exists, though most lean toward a common principal. The National Association of State Budget Officers (NASBO) provides the following brief explanation of how states identify spending for inclusion in the capital budget:

> States define the types of expenditures allowed in capital budgets to include such items as construction, improvements, land acquisition, site improvements, major renovations, and equipment. Definitions may also specify the anticipated useful life of a project and a minimum level of expenditure, with $25,000 being the most frequent minimum for capital budget expenditures.[8]

The ambiguity in some facets of this explanation is readily apparent. For example, the difference between a "major renovation" and a "minor renovation" may be arbitrary.

Nevertheless, the use of capital budgets and balanced budget rules makes it relatively difficult for state and local governments to issue debt to fund current operating expenses. Some states, however, do have some flexibility to shift spending between the operating and capital budgets, from fiscal year to fiscal year, and from account to account. This flexibility diminishes the seemingly disciplined treatment of debt. In addition, many states create and use special purpose authorities for debt issuance. These special authorities, though part of state government, are typically not constrained by the budget discipline tools described above.[9]

The Unemployment Trust Fund and Pension Debt

State and local governments also incur future liabilities that are not bonds. For example, many states borrow directly from the federal government to finance current expenditures for unemployment compensation (UC).[10] During recessions, the balance of these funds often falls to a point where states borrow to pay benefits. States can borrow from outside sources or from the federal government. As of February 18, 2011, 31 states and the U.S. Virgin Islands had borrowed a combined $43 billion through trust fund loans from the federal government.[11] These debts will be repaid through higher taxes on employers in most cases. A thorough examination of this type of debt and accompanying interest costs, though significant in some states, is beyond the scope of this report (for example, California owes over $10 billion to the federal government or 23% of the total outstanding).

Pension funds—in particular, defined benefit retirement funds—are also a significant liability or debt incurred by states and local governments. Recent studies have estimated that many state pensions are underfunded; one set the underfunding at $1 trillion.[12] As with UC programs, a thorough examination of this type of debt is beyond the scope of this report.

Holders of State and Local Government Debt

In addition to the discipline of budgetary rules, state and local government debt issuance is also constrained by the financial markets. As with any borrower, state and local governments need willing creditors to incur debt. The relative safety of state and local government debt and the federal income tax exclusion on interest payments on state and local bonds has created a strong demand for state and local government debt. What is also important to note is that entities that are otherwise non-taxable (or untaxable foreign entities) have little interest in tax-exempt state and local debt.

Individuals are the primary holders of state and local government debt. Figure 1 shows the holders of all outstanding municipal debt as of the fourth quarter of 2010.[13] Households, mutual funds, and money market funds represent holdings of individuals and compose approximately two-thirds (67%) of all debt outstanding. Individual holdings are represented in shades of blue. In past years, the individual share was larger as commercial banks and the rest of the world (ROW) held considerably less municipal debt. The recent increase in tax-exempt bond holdings by corporations and ROW can be attributed to the change in the more favorable tax treatment of corporate-held tax-exempt debt and Build America Bonds (BABs).[14] BABs are taxable and offer higher interest rates than tax-exempt bonds thus making them more attractive to non-taxable entities such as pension funds and international investors.

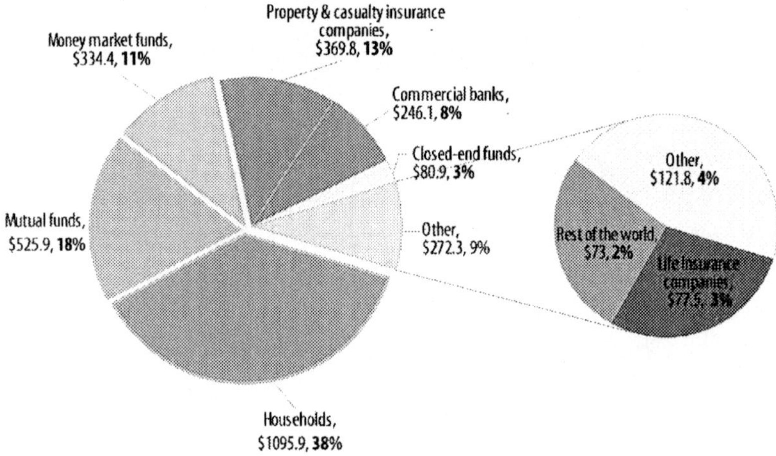

Source: CRS presentation of data from Federal Reserve Board, Flow of Funds Accounts, Flows and Outstandings, Fourth Quarter 2010.

Notes: The parts labeled "individuals" are chiefly owed by individuals directly or indirectly through the specified type of investment vehicle.

Figure 1. Holders of State and Local Government Debt Outstanding As of the Fourth Quarter of 2010 in Billions of Dollars.

The next section provides more detail on the level of state and local government debt. The discussion relies on data provided publicly by the Federal Reserve Board and U.S. Bureau of the Census and attempts to establish the current debt position of state and local governments and how it has changed over time.

MEASURING STATE AND LOCAL GOVERNMENT DEBT

The Fed and the United States Census Bureau (Census) publish information on state and local government debt outstanding. Both sources exhibit the relative importance of long-term debt. The Fed data are more current whereas the Census reports detailed data for both state and local government debt, albeit less current.

The Fed reports that, as of the third quarter of 2010, $2.39 trillion of state and local government debt was outstanding. Of this total, long-term debt composed 94.6%.[15] The Census reports that for FY2008, the latest year available, total state and local government outstanding debt was $2.55 trillion ($1 trillion in state debt and $1.55 trillion in local debt).[16] The Census further reports that in FY2008 *state* long-term debt was 98.6% of state total outstanding debt and *local* long-term debt was 98.0% of local total outstanding debt.

The amount of state and local government debt outstanding provides an indication of the relative magnitude of government borrowing. The government issuer, however, is not obligated to repay all of this debt; much of this debt is issued through debt vehicles called revenue bonds. Revenue bonds commit (or are secured by) a specified revenue stream, not the full faith and credit of the issuer. From 1996 through 2010, roughly one-third of state and local government debt issued was general obligation debt and two-thirds was specific revenue-secured debt.[17]

By comparison, total corporate and foreign bonds held by U.S. residents was $11.4 trillion at the close of the third quarter of 2010, and U.S. Treasury debt just recently reached $14.1 trillion.[18] Most corporate debt and all federal debt is backed by the full faith and credit of the issuer.

Relative Measures of State and Local Government Debt

The level of debt outstanding is best understood in the context of capacity to service that debt. One common measure of capacity to service debt is a jurisdiction's own-source revenue, excluding transfers from the federal government. This metric includes revenue from taxes (e.g., sales, income, and property) and revenue from fees and charges (e.g., public college tuition and recreation fees). It could be argued that own-source revenue may be the best metric to gauge capacity to service debt because state and local governments have a great deal of control over these revenue sources.

A narrower measure of capacity to service debt is using current tax revenue alone. Capacity would seem smaller using this measure and would make the local government situation look relatively more precarious as they rely less on current taxes and more on user charges and fees than state governments.

Table A-1 presents ratios measuring (1) debt to own-source revenue (presented in Figure 2) and (2) debt to current tax revenue for (a) state and local governments combined, (b) state governments alone, and (c) local governments alone for FY2008 (the latest available).[19] In states where local governments have less responsibility for government service provision, state level revenue and spending is a larger share of the total state and local government combined budget. In such states, the debt burden would lean more heavily on the state. With this in mind, the combined state and local government debt burden may be the best comparative measure across states.

The total state and local debt to taxes percentages should be viewed with caution as they may mask fundamental differences among states in how debt finance is shared between the state government and local governments. For example, total state and local government debt to taxes in New Hampshire and Tennessee are 212.1% and 188.3%, respectively. From this, one might conclude that, from a risk perspective, Tennessee's debt policies are relatively more sound than New Hampshire's. The state of New Hampshire does have the highest debt burden of all states (debt was 351% of taxes collected in FY2008) yet local governments in New Hampshire have the second lowest debt burden (debt was 97% of taxes collected). Whereas in Tennessee, the state had the lowest debt to taxes percentage of just 37.8%, but local governments in Tennessee had a debt to taxes percentage of 421.0%. Only five states had local governments with a higher debt-to-taxes percentage than Tennessee.

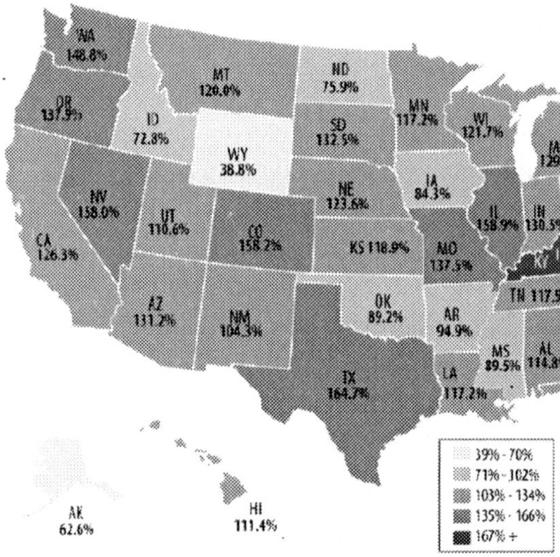

Source: United States Census Bureau, *State and Local Government Finances FY2008*, released July 2010.

Notes: See Table A-1 in the Appendix.

Figure 2. State and Local Debt Outstanding as Percent of Own-Source Revenue FY2008.

The difference between New Hampshire and Tennessee highlights how examining measures of state debt alone may understate potential debt strain at the sub-state government level. And, to the extent states may be indirectly responsible for the finances of sub-state governments, risk could be transferred from the local governments to state governments.

How Has State Debt Changed over Time?

The recession that began in December 2007 and ended June 2009 created significant fiscal strain on state and local governments.[20] The economy was in recession for over half of FY2008 and all of FY2009. Over this period, revenues declined and elevated spending intended to counter the effects of a slowed economy created what the National Association of State Budget Officers called "one of the worst periods in State fiscal conditions since the great depression."[21] In addition, federal assistance provided by the American Recovery and Reinvestment Act of 2009 is scheduled to expire and future pension obligations, for both retirement and health benefits, have created unease among many financial analysts and policymakers.

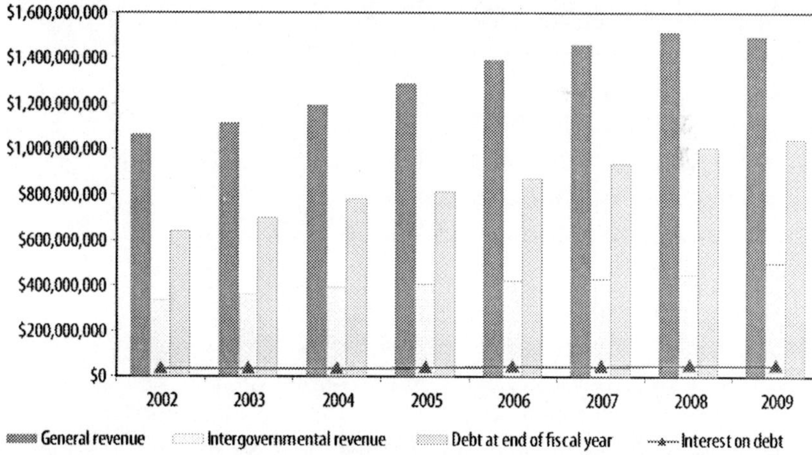

Source: CRS calculations based on United States Census Bureau, *State Government Finances: 2009*, available at http://www.census.gov/govs/state/.

Figure 3. Level of State Debt and General Revenue FY2002 to FY2009 in Current Dollars.

This section examines how state finances have changed over the FY2002 to FY2009 period. These years were selected for comparison because they are fairly representative of recent changing economic conditions. Both the beginning and end are considered economic troughs corresponding with the two most recent recessions. The recession of 2001 spanned from March 2001 to November 2001, which includes the beginning of FY2002 (for most states that would have been July 1, 2001). The data endpoint, FY2009, corresponds with the end of the most recent recession in June 2009.

Figure 3 shows the level of state general revenue, intergovernmental aid from the federal government, total state debt outstanding, and interest expense. The average annual growth rate for state debt outstanding over the period was 7.4% and total revenue, including intergovernmental aid, grew at an annual average rate of 2.2%. If intergovernmental aid were excluded, the average annual growth rate of state own-source revenue was 1.1% from 2002 to 2009.

The relatively continuous rise and slight drop in state general revenues in FY2009 is likely a key contributor to the current stress on state and local government operating budgets. State operating budgets, which as a general rule must be balanced from fiscal year to fiscal year, do not include *levels* of debt outstanding. The operating budget, however, does include interest payments on level of debt outstanding. These state interest payments outpaced state GDP growth over the same period, yet, as a portion of debt outstanding, declined from 5.2% to 4.5% from FY2002 to FY2009.

The lower (relative to state GDP) interest payments likely reflect falling interest rates over the last 20 years. In 1992, the average municipal bond rate was 6.41%, falling to 5.05% in 2002, and then to 4.64% in 2009.[22] As interest rates drop, states replace (or current refund) outstanding high interest rate bonds with lower interest rate bonds.[23] Also, any "new money" debt issuances carry a lower interest cost.

State Government Debt

Some policymakers have suggested that the level of state debt may grow, given the need to close current operating budget gaps, possibly with increased reliance on debt.[24] The budget gaps are relatively large from a historical perspective though state definitions of "deficit" vary considerably. The National Conference of State Legislatures (NCSL) estimates a FY2011 budget gap of $26.7 billion and a FY2012 budget gap of $82.1 billion.[25] States are generally reluctant to address gaps in the operating budget by reducing general fund spending that could be included in state capital budgets, which are financed primarily with debt. There is some evidence, however, to suggest that some states may have used this budget for financial flexibility. For example, despite the economic slowdown, capital spending increased 4.7% in FY2009, and was estimated to have grown 5.5% in FY2010.[26] This additional spending was financed with additional debt and federal funds.

In addition, the NASBO reports that 32.5% of spending on capital projects in FY2009 was financed with bonds. Other non-general fund sources, such as dedicated fees and fund surpluses, composed another 35.1% of capital spending. General fund financing of capital projects represented 5.9% and federal funds the remaining 26.5%. These levels reflect a change in the mix of funding sources. General fund financing of capital projects *decreased* by 35.9% whereas federal fund financing *increased* 15.3% and bond-financed spending *increased* 10.6%. The implication is that in recent years states may have relied more on debt financing of capital projects that in the past were paid with general fund revenues.

Many states, some researchers contend, may suffer from a so-called "fiscal illusion" that makes debt (or federal grants) appear to be "cheaper" than using general fund revenues. As a result, they argue, states spend more than they otherwise would if the spending were financed exclusively with general fund revenues. In times of budget stress, the incentives for using debt are even greater. Following is a brief discussion of research that has examined the tradeoff between financing spending with debt, federal aid, or current general fund revenues.

Fiscal Illusion and Debt versus Taxes

The fundamental question of how to finance expenditures settles on the choice between selling bonds or using current tax revenues. Fiscal illusion, as it applies to state and local government debt, refers to the perception of current taxpayers that public goods financed with debt are cheaper than using current taxes because payment is shifted to the future.[27] In theory, this illusion encourages more public spending than would otherwise be the case. This choice is principally a tradeoff between using taxes collected today versus taxes collected in the future.

Nevertheless, debt finance accomplishes two principal objectives of public finance. First, for debt issued for capital projects, the users of public infrastructure are repaying the debt through tax payments. This is typically called "pay-as-you-use" (payuse) financing and is considered more equitable as the taxpayers receiving the benefit are paying the taxes needed to repay the bond. Second, the use of debt smoothens spending on (often) large and expensive infrastructure projects. Without a bond issue, the jurisdiction would be required to make periodic lump sum payments for infrastructure. Accordingly, taxes would fluctuate as the payments are made.

Some jurisdictions, however, use a pay-as-you-go (paygo) system and "save" tax revenue and plan spending to match the saving and revenue structure. This requires a disciplined system of maintaining taxes and accurately anticipating future spending needs. One study concluded that ideally, a mix of the two financing mechanisms, depending on economic conditions, could maximize efficiency.[28] According to the study, during times of economic growth and budget surpluses, jurisdictions should use paygo and during economic downturns, payuse would be preferred. Stated differently, debt financed capital spending is more efficient during times of economic stress, and in time of surplus, using current revenue to finance capital spending is more efficient. This appears to reflect the recent experience.

Ricardian Equivalence and Debt Capitalization

One response to the fiscal illusion theory that suggests governments will borrow and spend "too much," is that the current generation will save more today in anticipation of the future taxes needed to repay the debt.[29] The theory presumes the current generation is interested in maintaining the consumption patterns of the next generation. To achieve this, the current generation saves and then transfers at death to the next generation an amount needed to retire debt incurred by the current generation. The net amount of debt would be unchanged. The list of restrictive assumptions needed to achieve the balance of planned saving to match debt repayment has led some to question the robustness of the so-called Ricardian Equivalence Model (REM).

A second response to the "over borrowing" critique relies on a model similar in principle to the REM. The debt capitalization model posits that future debt payments are "capitalized" into the value of property at the state and local government level.[30] In this theory, higher debt translates into lower property values as the market "capitalizes" or incorporates the requirement to repay future debt into the value of property today. As a result, the current generation "pays" for debt through lower property values today.

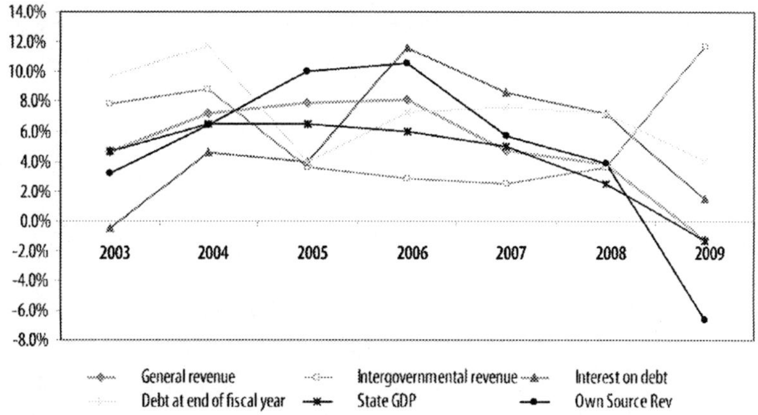

Source: CRS calculations based on United States Census Bureau, *State Government Finances*: 2009.

Notes: The data point for the year listed represents the change from the preceding fiscal year.

Figure 4. General Revenue Change from Previous Fiscal Year All States.

Change in State Debt from FY2002 to FY2009

As noted earlier, the last two recessions mark the beginning and end of the era examined. The level of state debt has increased from 59.9% of general revenue in FY2002 to 69.9% of general revenue in FY2009, and may increase further as the pace of the economic recovery and lagging housing market may continue to depress state (and local) revenue for FY2010, FY2011, and possibly FY2012. Figure 4 shows that general revenue growth actually declined in FY2009. The recession ended just before the beginning of FY2010 and the lag between economic decline and corresponding drop in revenues suggests that FY2010 may also exhibit a decline as well. State *tax* revenue, however, has shown recent improvement and may help alleviate some fiscal strain in FY2012.[31] Nevertheless, the growth in debt outstanding did slow, though it still exceeded general revenue growth the last three fiscal years.

Change in State Debt from FY2002 to FY2009, by State

The composite data for all states do not reflect significant differences among states. The variation in debt position across states can be measured as it relates to a common measure, such as personal income or general fund revenue or expenditures. For this report, both personal income and general fund expenditures are used to represent the "budget" capacity of the state. Even though a state may have the capacity as measured by personal income, the tax (and budget) structure is the mechanism through which the capacity is accessed. The interest expenditures of a state as a share of total expenditures provides a measure of a state's capacity to service debt out of the current operating budget.

Table A-2 exhibits two relative measures for FY2002 and FY2009 for each state. Figure 5 shows the FY2009 debt to personal income percentage for each state. The first is total debt outstanding as a share of personal income. In FY2009, total state debt as a share of personal income was 8.6%, up from 7.0% in FY2002. The increase likely reflects more debt as well as a decline in personal income in FY2009 given the severity of the recession. State debt as a share of personal income was over 21% in three states: Massachusetts, Alaska, and Rhode Island. In contrast, state debt in Nebraska, Texas, and Tennessee was below 4% of personal income. In addition, 12 states reduced debt as a share of personal income from FY2002 to FY2009. Overall, state debt outstanding has increased, though the overall debt position has been relatively stable for most states through FY2009.

The second set of data shows the relative importance of interest expense in state expenditures (excluding intergovernmental expenditures).[32] These data could be used as an indicator of the "affordability" of the debt load discussed above. As mentioned previously, debt is typically incurred for large capital projects and most (48) states use a separate capital budget to account for this debt. The state operating budget incorporates the capital budget through the interest expense, which appears as an expenditure in the operating budget. Total state interest expense in FY2002 and FY2009 was 4.5% of general fund expenditures.

OTHER STATE FISCAL STRAINS: PENSIONS AND DECLINING FEDERAL AID

Some have suggested that post-employment pensions for government workers are underfunded and compelling states to devote more revenue to shoring up pension funds. Recent reports have suggested that the amount needed to fully fund promised benefits could be as high as $1 trillion. For example, an analysis by the Pew Center on the States found that "at the end of fiscal year 2008, there was a $1 trillion gap between the $2.35 trillion states and participating localities had set aside to pay for employees' retirement benefits and the $3.35 trillion price tag of those promises."[33]

Future pension obligations, however, impact current operating deficits only to the extent that annual contributions will need to rise to fully fund pensions. Data for state and local governments for FY2008 show that government pension expenditures account for just under 3% of total expenditures or $82 billion for all state and local government pensions. These contributions are for future retirees. Payments for already retired or separated workers is a significantly larger expense ($180 billion in FY2008). These payments are funded through employee retirement trust funds, not from general fund revenue.

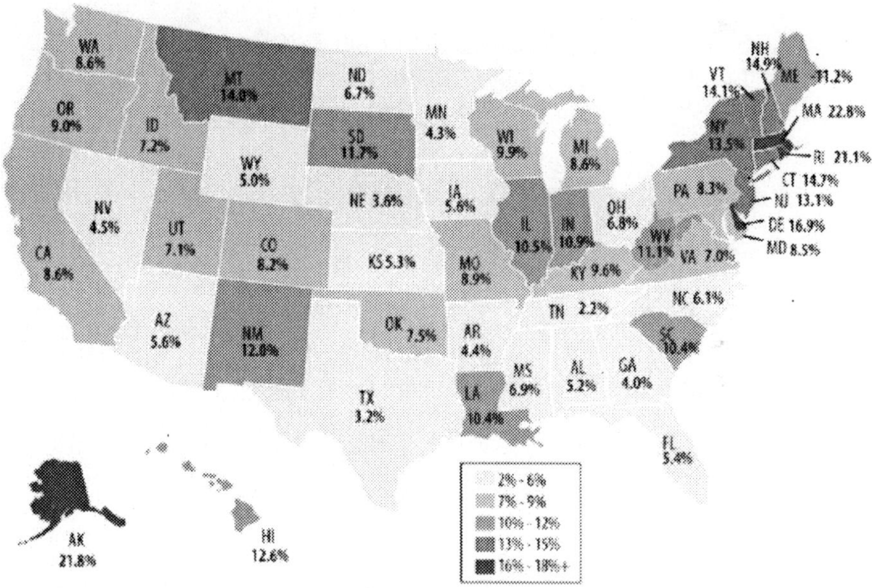

Source: CRS calculations based on U.S. Census Bureau Data, available at http://www.census.gov/govs/state/.

Notes: See Table A-2 in the Appendix.

Figure 5. State Debt as Percentage of State Personal Income FY2009.

Pension Obligation Bonds

Some governments have issued bonds to finance annual pension payments as a means to alleviate some fiscal strain. These bonds, called "pension obligation bonds" (POBs), are taxable and the issuing governments invest the proceeds of the POBs in the pension fund. The intent is for the return of the invested proceeds to exceed the interest cost on the bonds. The portion of pension assets funded with POBs is very small.[34] A recent study found that the "amount of POBs issued any one year has never been more than 1% of total assets in public pensions."[35] The same researchers concluded that

> Nevertheless, it appears that POBs have the potential to be useful tools in the hands of the right governments at the right time. Issuing a POB may allow well-heeled governments to gamble on the spread between interest rate costs and asset returns or to avoid raising taxes during a recession. Unfortunately, most often POB issuers are fiscally stressed and in a poor position to shoulder the investment risk. As such, most POBs appear to be issued by the wrong governments at the wrong time.[36]

Federal Aid

According to the United State Census Bureau, the federal government provided the states $497.8 billion in FY2009, or one-third of state general revenue.[37] NASBO reports that federal funds financed 29.5% of expenditures ($457.0 billion) in FY2009, rising to 34.7% ($563.7 billion) in FY2010.[38] As federal assistance contained in the American Recovery and Reinvestment Act (ARRA) gradually expires, the FY2011 federal share will likely decline somewhat. Currently, states are preparing the FY2012 budgets and are anticipating the need to increase revenue and reduce expenditures to replace the lost federal aid.

State Obligations: Debt and Unfunded Pension Liabilities

The amount of debt outstanding varies across states. The Census data presented in Table A-3 and Figure 6 do not differentiate among the types of debt that states issue. As noted above, some states include liabilities for future pension obligations while others do not.[39] As of the end of FY2009, states had issued over $1.04 trillion of debt compared to $1.5 trillion in state general revenue.[40] As shown in Figure 6 (and Table A-3), state debt ranged from $1.3 billion in Wyoming to $134.5 billion in California. The national average was $20.9 billion.

According to the Pew Center on the States, at the end of FY2008, total unfunded pension liabilities were $449 billion and unfunded health benefits amounted to $555 billion. Summing the two post-employment liabilities of government with debt provides a more complete picture of each state's future obligations. Hawaii and New Jersey, with debt and unfunded pension obligations of 34.4% and 33.2% of state GDP respectively, significantly exceed the national average of 14.5%. In contrast, Tennessee and Wyoming had debt and unfunded obligations of 3.4% and 4.4% of GDP, respectively. Recall, however, (see Table A-1) that local governments in Tennessee carry a relatively large share of the debt burden in that state.

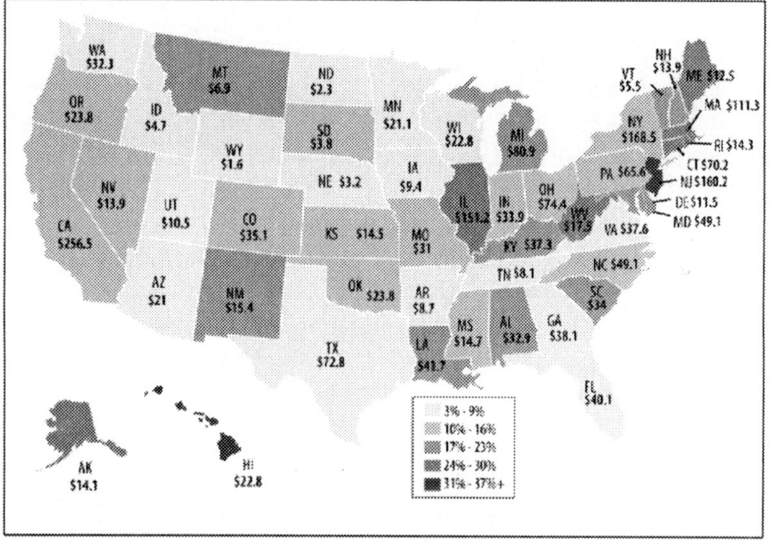

Source: CRS Calculations based on U.S. Census Bureau, *State Government Finances 2009*; and Pew Center on the States, "The Trillion Dollar Gap: Underfunded State Retirement Systems and the Roads to Reform," February 2010.

Notes: The bond debt is at the end of FY2009. The unfunded pension data are for FY2008. See Table A-3 in the Appendix.

Figure 6. State Debt and Unfunded Pension Liabilities as Percent of State GDP Amount in Billions of Dollars.

Economics of State and Local Government Debt

The use of public debt has important economic consequences that extend beyond the comparative metrics presented in this report. Economists examine broader issues surrounding government debt and its impact on the financial markets and the economy. These issues, which are not mutually exclusive, include (1) the degree to which government debt crowds out domestic investment and net exports and (2) the economic efficiency of using tax-exempt debt to subsidize public capital formation. The two chiefly negative consequences may seem to justify greater oversight of state and local government debt and the implicit federal subsidy. Designing a federal oversight role, however, would need to address the underlying constitutional issues governing the federal-state relationship.

Crowding out of Domestic Investment and Net Exports

In a typical economic model, the level of savings in the economy is equal to investment and is fixed over time. Under this model, when governments borrow, those savings are not available for private domestic investment, raising interest rates and making private borrowing more expensive. The higher interest rate also leads to net inflows of foreign capital as investors look to invest in the United States. The dollar would strengthen resulting in a drop in net exports as dollar-denominated goods become more expensive.

State and local government debt, thus, is often seen as having a significant impact on the macroeconomy, and some economists argue that if state government borrowing becomes "excessive" that borrowing could have a negative impact on private domestic investment and net exports.[41] As such, the economic impact of state and local government debt issuance is generally perceived as of congressional interest as is the role of the federal government in either promoting or impeding the issuance of state debt.[42]

Economic Efficiency of Tax-Exempt Debt

The federal government currently provides a tax preference for state and local government debt.[43] The latest estimate of the federal tax expenditure for tax-exempt state and local government debt is $161.6 billion over the 2010 to 2014 forecast window.[44] This tax expenditure is the direct cost to the federal government of the exclusion of interest paid on state and local government debt from individual and corporate income taxes.

The tax preference provided through tax-exempt bonds, however, has been criticized as "not a cost-effective means of transferring resources from the federal government to state and local governments."[45] Congress may act to more fully explore alternatives to tax-exempt financing considering the volume of tax-exempt financing and the economic inefficiency. Following is a brief discussion of why tax-exempt bonds are seen as an economically inefficient means of federal assistance to state and local governments.

Consider a 35% marginal tax rate investor who purchases a 5% tax-exempt bond with principal amount of $1 million to be repaid over 20 years. Each year for 20 years this taxpayer receives $50,000 in tax-exempt interest income. Each year the federal government forgoes collecting $24,500 (investor tax rate multiplied by what the taxable interest would have been) of revenue because the revenue loss is based upon the yield the taxpayer forgoes (the taxable yield) and the taxes that would have been collected on that interest income. For example, if the investor had purchased a taxable bond carrying a 7% interest rate, he would have received $70,000 in interest income and paid $24,500 in income taxes on that income (35% times $70,000).[46]

The previous example presents the fundamental economic inefficiency of tax-exempt bonds. The after-tax rate of return for the tax-exempt bond is the full 5% ($50,000 divided by $1 million). The after-tax rate of return for the taxable bond is 4.55% ($45,500 divided by $1 million). Theoretically, the federal government is providing an additional $4,500 to this investor for purchasing the tax-exempt bond.

Also, consider that the issuer is receiving a subsidy through lower interest costs. In this example, the issuer receives a two-percentage-point (the difference between a taxable rate of 7% and a tax-exempt rate of 5%) discount on debt or $20,000 which is less than the $24,500 tax expenditure. In theory, the federal government could provide the issuer with a direct subsidy of up to $24,500 to the issuer yielding a smaller revenue loss.

Over time, the size of the federal subsidy for state and local government debt issuance has varied along with macroeconomic factors and more directly with the marginal income tax rates. The historical average interest rate on high-grade corporate bonds from 1939 to 2010 was 6.26% and for high-grade municipal debt, 4.89%. In 2010, the average was 4.94% for corporate debt and 4.16% for municipal debt.[47] The relatively high municipal bond rate in 2010, 0.84 of the taxable rate, confers a significant tax preference to higher tax rate investors.

CONGRESSIONAL ACTION

This report examines the complexities of state and local government finance and how the magnitude of state fiscal stress varies considerably from state to state. Congress has recently held hearings examining the fiscal health of state and local governments and has offered legislation in two areas related to state and local fiscal health analyzed in this report: government debt and government pensions.

State and local debt, although growing, has not reached the point where widespread default seems likely. To date, few defaults have occurred and interest costs for debt outstanding represented a relatively modest 3.5% of total state and local government expenditures (4.5% of state expenditures in FY2009). More recent government budget data may show that for selected local government issuers, such as governmental authorities that rely on specialized revenue streams, interest costs have risen and default—and possible state government intervention—may be more likely than in the past. Prolonged weakness in the economy would certainly raise this probability.

Some policymakers are concerned that state and local governments are issuing too much debt, increasing the risk of potential default. In response, Congress may seek to increase oversight of the municipal bond market. Historically, the federal government has not actively engaged in regulating how state and local governments finance activities.[48] Congress has limited authority as the Tower Amendment to the Securities and Exchange Act of 1934 explicitly prohibits the federal government from requiring

> any issuer of municipal securities, directly or indirectly through a purchaser or prospective purchaser of securities from the issuer, to file with the [Securities and Exchange] Commission or the [Municipal Securities Rulemaking] Board prior to the sale of such securities by the issuer any application, report, or document in connection with the issuance, sale, or distribution of such securities.[49]

Congress does confer a tax preference to state and local government bond issuers and could modify this tax preference to induce changes in bond disclosure requirements. Also, the Internal Revenue Service (IRS) currently audits selected outstanding tax-exempt bond issues to determine if the bonds comply with tax law. Expanding these audits may help ensure that the tax-exemption and associated federal revenue loss is merited.

Congress may also examine alternatives to tax-exempt bonds for subsidizing state and local government capital investment. In the 112th Congress, several bills have been introduced to extend and expand a modified version of Build America Bonds (BABs) including H.R. 11, H.R. 736, H.R. 747, and H.R. 992. BABs are viewed by many observers as a more efficient alternative to tax-exempt bonds.

Congress may also take a more active role in the oversight of state and local government pensions. Legislation has been introduced to address state pension issues. H.R. 567 and S. 347 would require greater transparency of state and local government pension systems. Recently, Moody's, one of the primary bond rating agencies, announced that it would begin integrating tax-supported debt and unfunded pension liabilities when evaluating state bond ratings.[50]

In the near term, however, annual pension costs represent roughly 3% of state and local government operating expenditures ($82 billion in FY2008). As such, the underfunded pension systems are a longer term concern and, for most states, have a marginal impact on short term operating deficits.

APPENDIX

Table A-1. Relative Measure of State and Local Government Debt Outstanding FY2008

State	Debt Outstanding as Percentage of Own Source Revenue, FY2008			Debt Outstanding as Percentage of Tax Revenues, FY2008		
	State and Local	State	Local	State and Local	State	Local
United States Total	131.2%	94.0%	176.4%	191.7%	128.5%	281.9%
Alabama	114.8%	59.4%	192.8%	199.5%	93.4%	393.1%
Alaska	62.6%	47.4%	156.0%	102.3%	77.1%	264.7%
Arizona	131.2%	57.8%	220.3%	189.6%	76.8%	356.0%
Arkansas	94.9%	41.9%	253.7%	137.6%	56.9%	461.6%
California	126.3%	85.6%	171.6%	183.4%	103.9%	319.2%
Colorado	158.2%	108.4%	201.3%	254.5%	165.0%	340.5%

Table A-1. (Continued)

State	Debt Outstanding as Percentage of Own Source Revenue, FY2008			Debt Outstanding as Percentage of Tax Revenues, FY2008		
	State and Local	State	Local	State and Local	State	Local
Connecticut	132.8%	155.5%	92.5%	159.2%	188.8%	108.4%
Delaware	121.3%	109.4%	168.0%	213.9%	195.3%	284.1%
District of Columbia	136.6%	0.0%	136.6%	177.5%	0.0%	177.5%
Florida	126.0%	88.5%	153.6%	193.8%	118.1%	266.1%
Georgia	101.4%	55.4%	142.7%	150.3%	72.3%	240.9%
Hawaii	111.4%	83.6%	204.2%	155.0%	117.1%	277.9%
Idaho	72.8%	71.0%	75.5%	116.0%	92.5%	182.5%
Illinois	158.9%	144.2%	174.7%	214.7%	183.2%	253.3%
Indiana	130.5%	95.3%	180.1%	202.8%	131.8%	339.8%
Iowa	84.3%	69.7%	103.4%	133.9%	105.0%	176.8%
Kansas	118.9%	58.3%	198.2%	176.6%	81.5%	320.8%
Kentucky	181.0%	85.9%	374.2%	271.2%	121.4%	638.6%
Louisiana	117.2%	104.5%	134.5%	177.6%	148.9%	223.1%
Maine	96.6%	101.3%	87.8%	131.4%	139.9%	116.4%
Maryland	102.8%	108.4%	95.2%	137.3%	146.8%	124.8%
Massachusetts	194.6%	227.8%	129.7%	273.0%	328.1%	173.2%
Michigan	129.2%	81.2%	205.7%	199.9%	117.3%	358.9%
Minnesota	117.2%	42.5%	244.8%	168.5%	52.1%	501.5%
Mississippi	89.5%	71.9%	115.1%	144.7%	93.5%	286.8%
Missouri	137.5%	125.4%	150.8%	206.9%	179.7%	240.4%
Montana	120.0%	137.9%	85.0%	187.7%	200.3%	156.3%
Nebraska	123.6%	46.9%	204.0%	186.6%	64.3%	344.4%
Nevada	158.0%	56.3%	251.4%	235.2%	69.5%	461.7%
New Hampshire	146.5%	204.0%	79.1%	212.1%	351.3%	96.5%
New Jersey	126.0%	131.4%	118.7%	163.5%	172.4%	151.8%
New Mexico	104.3%	82.7%	165.6%	171.1%	137.5%	261.2%
New York	146.5%	132.2%	159.1%	195.1%	174.8%	213.3%
North Carolina	103.7%	66.6%	158.5%	154.2%	86.1%	303.0%
North Dakota	75.9%	57.0%	122.2%	115.2%	84.4%	197.7%

State	Debt Outstanding as Percentage of Own Source Revenue, FY2008			Debt Outstanding as Percentage of Tax Revenues, FY2008		
	State and Local	State	Local	State and Local	State	Local
Ohio	100.2%	72.0%	133.9%	147.1%	102.9%	203.5%
Oklahoma	89.2%	75.3%	113.7%	137.6%	109.6%	196.1%
Oregon	137.9%	98.6%	186.8%	234.7%	160.0%	338.3%
Pennsylvania	154.2%	89.9%	243.1%	219.2%	124.8%	357.1%
Rhode Island	165.1%	207.3%	95.4%	233.8%	322.7%	117.6%
South Carolina	150.6%	112.7%	198.2%	277.7%	190.7%	411.7%
South Dakota	132.5%	157.1%	102.8%	209.9%	257.9%	156.0%
Tennessee	117.9%	25.9%	232.9%	188.3%	37.8%	421.0%
Texas	164.7%	50.9%	277.7%	249.9%	74.5%	437.8%
Utah	110.6%	60.6%	201.1%	178.5%	96.7%	331.7%
Vermont	106.3%	98.1%	149.3%	147.9%	132.5%	247.9%
Virginia	112.6%	76.1%	165.3%	167.2%	118.8%	229.6%
Washington	148.8%	98.1%	211.5%	225.8%	131.0%	385.9%
West Virginia	97.0%	85.1%	130.7%	153.0%	130.4%	224.5%
Wisconsin	121.7%	105.5%	146.5%	172.8%	146.5%	215.6%
Wyoming	38.8%	38.8%	38.9%	63.5%	55.8%	77.8%

Source: United States Census Bureau, *State and Local Government Finances FY2008*, released July 2010.

Notes: Note that the data released debt in Wyoming did not meet the Total Quantity Response Rates for the Census Bureau's 70% standard.

Table A-2. Change in State Debt and Interest Expense from FY2002 to FY2009 Debt as Share of Personal Income and Interest as Share of General Fund Expenditures

State	Debt to Personal Income			Interest Cost as Share of General Fund Expenditures		
	FY2002	FY2009	Change	FY2002	FY2009	Change
United States	7.0%	8.6%	1.5%	4.5%	4.5%	0.0%
Alabama	5.5%	5.2%	-0.4%	2.0%	2.0%	0.0%
Alaska	24.9%	21.8%	-3.1%	5.0%	3.7%	-1.2%
Arizona	2.9%	5.6%	2.7%	1.9%	2.8%	0.9%
Arkansas	4.6%	4.4%	-0.2%	1.8%	1.6%	-0.2%

Table A-2. (Continued)

State	Debt to Personal Income			Interest Cost as Share of General Fund Expenditures		
	FY2002	FY2009	Change	FY2002	FY2009	Change
California	6.0%	8.6%	2.6%	4.7%	5.4%	0.6%
Colorado	4.5%	8.2%	3.6%	3.4%	5.8%	2.4%
Connecticut	13.9%	14.7%	0.8%	8.2%	8.4%	0.2%
Delaware	15.1%	16.9%	1.8%	7.5%	5.2%	-2.3%
Florida	4.0%	5.4%	1.4%	3.2%	3.4%	0.3%
Georgia	3.3%	4.0%	0.7%	2.2%	2.6%	0.4%
Hawaii	15.1%	12.6%	-2.5%	7.1%	4.4%	-2.7%
Idaho	7.3%	7.2%	-0.1%	4.4%	3.6%	-0.8%
Illinois	8.2%	10.5%	2.3%	6.2%	7.1%	0.8%
Indiana	5.4%	10.9%	5.5%	2.8%	4.4%	1.5%
Iowa	4.4%	5.6%	1.2%	1.5%	2.2%	0.7%
Kansas	2.8%	5.3%	2.5%	1.9%	3.5%	1.6%
Kentucky	6.8%	9.6%	2.8%	3.5%	2.9%	-0.6%
Louisiana	8.0%	10.4%	2.4%	4.3%	4.5%	0.2%
Maine	11.6%	11.2%	-0.3%	5.1%	4.2%	-0.9%
Maryland	6.1%	8.5%	2.4%	4.6%	4.5%	-0.1%
Massachusetts	17.8%	22.8%	5.0%	12.3%	11.7%	-0.7%
Michigan	7.2%	8.6%	1.4%	4.3%	3.7%	-0.6%
Minnesota	3.7%	4.3%	0.5%	2.3%	3.2%	0.8%
Mississippi	6.3%	6.9%	0.6%	2.6%	1.8%	-0.8%
Missouri	7.6%	8.9%	1.3%	4.2%	4.5%	0.3%
Montana	11.8%	14.0%	2.3%	5.0%	4.0%	-0.9%
Nebraska	4.2%	3.6%	-0.7%	2.5%	1.7%	-0.8%
Nevada	5.4%	4.5%	-0.9%	3.9%	3.5%	-0.4%
New Hampshire	12.1%	14.9%	2.8%	10.7%	8.6%	-2.2%
New Jersey	9.4%	13.1%	3.7%	5.1%	5.8%	0.7%
New Mexico	9.7%	12.0%	2.3%	3.0%	3.0%	0.0%
New York	13.0%	13.5%	0.5%	8.0%	7.0%	-1.0%
North Carolina	4.7%	6.1%	1.4%	2.9%	2.2%	-0.7%
North Dakota	9.7%	6.7%	-3.0%	3.9%	4.7%	0.8%
Ohio	5.9%	6.8%	0.9%	4.2%	3.9%	-0.3%
Oklahoma	7.1%	7.5%	0.4%	3.5%	3.6%	0.1%
Oregon	7.3%	9.0%	1.7%	2.3%	3.3%	1.0%
Pennsylvania	5.4%	8.3%	2.9%	3.1%	4.0%	0.9%
Rhode Island	17.1%	21.1%	4.0%	6.3%	8.7%	2.5%
South Carolina	9.5%	10.4%	0.9%	6.1%	4.5%	-1.6%
South Dakota	10.8%	11.7%	0.9%	5.9%	4.5%	-1.4%
Tennessee	2.2%	2.2%	0.0%	1.4%	1.2%	-0.2%
Texas	3.3%	3.2%	-0.1%	2.0%	1.8%	-0.2%
Utah	7.9%	7.1%	-0.8%	2.7%	2.2%	-0.4%
Vermont	13.4%	14.1%	0.8%	5.6%	4.7%	-1.0%

State	Debt to Personal Income			Interest Cost as Share of General Fund Expenditures		
	FY2002	FY2009	Change	FY2002	FY2009	Change
Virginia	5.6%	7.0%	1.4%	4.2%	3.5%	-0.7%
Washington	6.8%	8.6%	1.8%	3.7%	4.2%	0.5%
West Virginia	10.3%	11.1%	0.8%	3.9%	3.0%	-0.9%
Wisconsin	8.9%	9.9%	1.0%	5.4%	6.3%	0.9%
Wyoming	8.1%	5.0%	-3.1%	4.4%	2.1%	-2.3%

Source: CRS calculations based on U.S. Census Bureau Data.

Notes: The general fund expenditures do not include contributions to insurance funds on behalf of employees.

Table A-3. State Debt and Unfunded Pension Obligations Amounts in Thousands of Dollars

State	Debt at End of FY2009	Unfunded Pension Obligation FY2008[a]	Unfunded Healthcare and Non-Obligation FY2008[b]	Total Debt and Pension Obligations FY2009	Total Debt as Portion of State GDP
United States	$1,044,035,3 80	$448,895,687	$555,102,484	$2,048,033,551	14.5%
Alabama	8,155,943	9,228,918	15,549,411	32,934,272	19.4%
Alaska	6,589,698	3,522,661	4,032,052	14,144,411	30.9%
Arizona	12,324,879	7,871,120	808,818	21,004,817	8.2%
Arkansas	4,135,051	2,752,546	1,822,241	8,709,838	8.6%
California	134,571,934	59,492,498	62,463,000	256,527,432	13.6%
Colorado	17,202,374	16,813,048	1,127,179	35,142,601	13.9%
Connecticut	28,394,151	15,858,500	26,018,800	70,271,451	30.9%
Delaware	5,984,645	129,359	5,409,600	11,523,604	19.0%
Florida	38,885,422	(1,798,789)	3,081,834	40,168,467	5.4%
Georgia	13,455,164	6,384,903	18,322,123	38,162,190	9.7%
Hawaii	6,880,242	5,168,108	10,791,300	22,839,650	34.4%
Idaho	3,508,973	772,200	489,421	4,770,594	8.8%
Illinois	56,962,364	54,383,939	39,946,678	151,292,981	24.0%
Indiana	23,711,889	9,825,830	442,268	33,979,987	12.9%
Iowa	6,353,306	2,694,794	404,300	9,452,400	6.6%
Kansas	5,857,295	8,279,168	316,640	14,453,103	11.6%
Kentucky	13,364,138	12,328,429	11,660,245	37,352,812	23.9%
Louisiana	17,504,772	11,658,734	12,542,953	41,706,459	20.0%
Maine	5,396,983	2,782,173	4,347,702	12,526,858	24.4%
Maryland	23,472,579	10,926,099	14,723,420	49,122,098	17.1%
Massach-usetts	74,597,901	21,759,452	15,031,600	111,388,953	30.5%
Michigan	29,591,278	11,514,600	39,878,500	80,984,378	22.0%

Table A-3. (Continued)

State	Debt at End of FY2009	Unfunded Pension Obligation FY2008[a]	Unfunded Healthcare and Non-Obligation FY2008[b]	Total Debt and Pension Obligations FY2009	Total Debt as Portion of State GDP
Minnesota	9,392,931	10,771,507	1,011,400	21,175,838	8.1%
Mississippi	6,208,639	7,971,277	570,248	14,750,164	15.4%
Missouri	19,217,206	9,025,293	2,851,826	31,094,325	13.0%
Montana	4,763,503	1,549,503	631,918	6,944,924	19.3%
Nebraska	2,516,775	754,748	na	3,271,523	3.8%
Nevada	4,444,804	7,281,752	2,211,439	13,937,995	11.0%
New Hampshire	8,411,660	2,522,175	3,054,188	13,988,023	23.5%
New Jersey	56,897,866	34,434,055	68,900,000	160,231,921	33.2%
New Mexico	8,001,721	4,519,887	2,946,290	15,467,898	20.7%
New York	122,651,630	(10,428,000)	56,286,000	168,509,630	15.4%
North Carolina	19,910,714	504,760	28,741,560	49,157,034	12.3%
North Dakota	1,752,558	546,500	81,276	2,380,334	7.5%
Ohio	27,949,184	19,502,065	27,025,738	74,476,987	15.8%
Oklahoma	9,855,393	13,172,407	359,800	23,387,600	15.2%
Oregon	12,494,686	10,739,000	609,793	23,843,479	14.4%
Pennsyl-vania	41,924,042	13,724,480	9,956,800	65,605,322	11.8%
Rhode Island	9,180,938	4,353,892	788,189	14,323,019	29.9%
South Carolina	15,313,021	10,052,684	8,638,076	34,003,781	21.3%
South Dakota	3,626,024	182,870	76,406	3,885,300	10.1%
Tennessee	4,847,786	1,602,802	1,746,879	8,197,467	3.4%
Texas	30,438,160	13,781,228	28,611,584	72,830,972	6.4%
Utah	6,267,888	3,611,399	672,843	10,552,130	9.3%
Vermont	3,426,670	461,551	1,614,581	5,502,802	21.6%
Virginia	24,301,179	10,723,000	2,621,000	37,645,179	9.2%
Washington	24,603,219	(179,100)	7,901,610	32,325,729	9.6%
West Virginia	6,501,995	4,968,709	6,108,398	17,579,102	27.8%
Wisconsin	20,913,355	252,600	1,700,396	22,866,351	9.4%
Wyoming	1,320,852	144,353	174,161	1,639,366	4.4%

Source: CRS Calculations based on U.S. Census Bureau, *State Government Finances 2009*; and Pew Center on the States, "The Trillion Dollar Gap: Underfunded State Retirement Systems and the Roads to Reform," February 2010.

Notes: The Pew Center pension data are from FY2008. As most pensions are heavily invested, the data do not reflect the sharp decline in assets value in the last half of 2008 and in 2009. Thus, the underfunding should be viewed as a conservative estimate.

a. Data are estimates from *Pew Center on the States*, 2010.

b. Data are estimates from *Pew Center on the States*, 2010.

End Notes

[1] An overview of some techniques used to "manage" state budget constraints can be found in the following: Eileen Norcross, *Fiscal Evasion in State Budgeting*, Mercatus Center, George Mason University, Working Paper no. 10-39, July 2010.

[2] For more on the history, see Moody's Investor Service, "U.S. Municipal Bond defaults and Recoveries, 1970-2009," February 2010. As for future defaults, though difficult to predict, the Bond Dealers of America reports that "in the last four years and during the height of the recession, only seven municipal governments filed for bankruptcy." See Mike Nicholas, Chief Executive Officer, Bond Dealers of America, as reported in the *The Bond Buyer*, February 28, 2011.

[3] James B. Burnham, "Risky Business?: Evaluating the Use of Pension Obligations Bonds," *Government Finance Review*, June 2003, p. 12-17.

[4] For more on state and local government debt, see CRS Report RL30638, *Tax-Exempt Bonds: A Description of State and Local Government Debt*, by Steven Maguire.

[5] U.S. Congress, Senate Committee on the Budget, *Challenges for the U.S. Economy*, 112th Cong., 1st sess., February 3, 2011; U.S. Congress, House Committee on Oversight and Government Reform, Subcommittee on TARP, Financial Services and Bailouts of Public and Private Programs, *State and Municipal Debt: The Coming Crisis?*, 112th Cong., 1st sess., February 9, 2011; and U.S. Congress, House Committee on Oversight and Government Reform, Subcommittee on TARP, Financial Services and Bailouts of Public and Private Programs, *State and Municipal Debt: The Coming Crisis? Part II*, 112th Cong., 1st sess., March 15, 2011. U.S. Congress, House Committee on Oversight and Government Reform, *State and Municipal Debt: Tough Choices Ahead*, 112th Cong., 1st sess., April 14, 2011.

[6] National Association of State Budget Officers (NASBO), "Budget Processes in the States," Washington, DC, Summer 2008, available at *http://www.nasbo.org/LinkClick .aspx?fileticket=AaAKTnjgucg%3d&tabid=38*.

[7] NASBO, "Capital Budgeting in the States," Washington, DC, November 1999, available at http://www.nasbo.org/ LinkClick.aspx?fileticket=yfDocTSXHU4=&tabid=84.

[8] NASBO, "Capital Budgeting in the States," 1999, p. 8.

[9] An overview of some techniques used to "manage" state budget constraints can be found in the following: Eileen Norcross, *Fiscal Evasion in State Budgeting*, Mercatus Center, George Mason University, Working Paper no. 10-39, July 2010.

[10] CRS Report RS22954, *The Unemployment Trust Fund (UTF): State Insolvency and Federal Loans to States*, by Julie M. Whittaker.

[11] United States Department of Labor, Employment and Training Administration, "Trust Fund Loans," Washington, DC, available at *http://www.workforcesecurity.doleta.gov/unemploy* /budget.asp#tfloans, visited February 23, 2011.

[12] Pew Center for the States, "The Trillion Dollar Gap: Underfunded State Retirement Systems and the Road to Reform," Washington, DC, February 2010, available at *http://downloads* .pewcenteronthestates.org/ The_Trillion_Dollar_Gap_final.pdf.

[13] This total includes the debt issued by nonprofit organizations and nonfinancial businesses.

[14] For further analysis of Build America Bonds, see CRS Report R40523, *Tax Credit Bonds: Overview and Analysis*, by Steven Maguire.

[15] Federal Reserve Board, "Flow of Funds Accounts, Flows and Outstandings, Third Quarter 2010," available at http://www.federalreserve.gov/releases/z1/. This total does not include the amounts issued by nonprofit organizations and nonfinancial corporate businesses.

[16] United States Census Bureau, *State and Local Government Finances FY2008*, released July 7, 2010. The Fed reports $2.68 trillion outstanding for 2008

[17] Thomson-Reuters as provided by the Securities Industry and Financial Markets Association (SIFMA). Data available at http://www.sifma.org/research/statistics.aspx.

[18] For more on Treasury debt outstanding, see CRS Report RL31967, *The Debt Limit: History and Recent Increases*, by D. Andrew Austin and Mindy R. Levit.

[19] The FY2008 data, though somewhat dated, are still informative for comparative analysis. Debt outstanding does not fluctuate drastically from year to year as most of the underlying debt is long term. The drop in revenues corresponding with the 2007 to 2009 recession, however, is not reflected in the percentages.

[20] National Bureau of Economic Research, "U.S. Business Cycle Expansions and Contractions," available at http://www.nber.org/cycles/cyclesmain.html, visited January 31, 2011.

[21] NASBO, "The Fiscal Survey of States: Fall 2010," Washington, DC, p. vii., available at http://www.nasbo.org/ LinkClick.aspx?fileticket=EQnlICsAJD8%3d&tabid=38.

[22] Office of Management and Budget, "Economic Report of the President," Table B-73, February 2011. The interest rate dropped further in 2010 to 4.16%.

[23] Municipal bonds typically include a 10-year call provision where the issuer can buy back outstanding debt.

[24] For a discussion, see U.S. Congress, House Committee on Oversight and Government Reform, Subcommittee on TARP, Financial Services and Bailouts of Public and Private Programs, *State and Municipal Debt: The Coming Crisis*, 112th Cong., 1st sess., February 19, 2011.

[25] National Conference of State Legislatures, "NCSL Fiscal Brief: Top Fiscal Issues for 2011 Legislative Sessions," January 3, 2011, p. 1.

[26] All expenditure data are from the National Association of State Budget Officers, "Fiscal Year 2009 State Expenditure Report," Fall 2010. The report is available at *http://www .nasbo.org/*.

[27] A singular definition of "fiscal illusion" does not exist. J. Buchanan, *Public Finance in Democratic Process*, University of North Carolina Press, 1967.

[28] Wen Wang and Yilin Hou, "Pay-as-You-Go Financing and Capital Outlay Volatility: Evidence from the States over Two Recent Economic Cycles," *Public Budgeting and Finance*, vol. 29, no. 4, 2009, pp. 90-107.

[29] Barro, R.J., "Are Government Bonds Net Wealth?," *Journal of Political Economy*, vol. 82, no. 6, 1974, pp. 1095-1117.

[30] These applications are relevant for state and local governments more so than federal level governments. For more, see Eichenberger, Reiner, and David Stadelman, "How Federalism Protects Future Generations from Today's Public Debts," *Review of Law and Economics*, vol. 6, no. 3, 2010; and Banzahaf, H.S., and W.E. Oates, "On Ricardian Equivalence in Local Public Finance," June 2008, available at http://ssrn.com/abstract=1248002.

[31] Tax revenue is obviously the most important component of general revenue, yet composed just 48% of the total. Dadayan, Lucy and Donald Boyd, "State Tax Revenues Rebound Further, Growing For Third Straight Quarter," The Nelson A. Rockefeller Institute of Government, *State Revenue Flash Report*, November 30, 2010. Available at *http://www.rockinst* .org/pdf/government_finance/state_revenue_report/2010-11-30-State_Revenue_Flash.pdf.

[32] These expenditures are sometimes referred to as "general fund" expenditures.

[33] The Pew Center on the States, "The Trillion Dollar Gap: Underfunded State Retirement Systems and the Roads to Reform," February 2010, available at http://downloads.pewcenteronthestates.org/The_Trillion_Dollar_Gap_final.pdf.

[34] Illinois, however, offered $3.7 billion of pension obligation bonds on March 10, 2011.

[35] Munnell, Alicia, Thad Calabrese, Ashby Monk, and Jean-Peirre Aubry, "Pension Obligation Bonds: Financial Crisis Exposes Risks," Center for State and Local Government Excellence, January 2010, p. 7. Available at *http://www.slge.org/vertical/Sites* /%7BA260E1DF-5AEE-459D-84C4-876EFE1E4032%7D/uploads/%7BD84F0CBF-78F0-41C1-93ED-84CACA92DE48%7D.PDF.

[36] Ibid.

[37] U.S. Census Bureau, "State Government Finances: 2009," January 5, 2011.

[38] National Association of State Budget Officers, "Fiscal Year 2009 State Expenditure Report," Fall 2010. The report is available at http://www.nasbo.org/.

[39] The Government Finance Officers Association (GFOA) recommends that issuers only include the following types of debt in a debt management policy: direct debt which is payable from general revenues, including capital leases; revenue debt which is payable from a specific pledged revenue source; conduit debt, which is payable by third parties for which the government does not provide credit or security, state revolving loan funds and pools; other types of hybrid debt, which is payable from special revenues or containing other unique security pledges; and interfund borrowing, which are loans for short-term cash flow needs.

[40] General revenue does not include state pension net revenue, state owned utility company revenue, and state owned liquor store revenue.

[41] This holds for all government debt, not just state and local government debt.

[42] Aizenman, Joshua, and Gurnail Kaur Pasricha, "Net Fiscal Stimulus During the Great Recession," *National Bureau of Economic Research*, no. 16779, February 2011.

[43] CRS Report RL30638, *Tax-Exempt Bonds: A Description of State and Local Government Debt*, by Steven Maguire.

[44] U.S. Congress, Joint Committee on Taxation, "Estimates of Federal Tax Expenditures for Fiscal Years 2010 to 2014," JCS-3-10, December 10, 2010.

[45] Donald B. Marron, Acting Director of the U.S. Congressional Budget Office, *Economic Issues in the Use of Tax-Preferred Financing*, Testimony before the Committee on Ways and Means, Subcommittee on Select Revenue Measures, March 16, 2006.

[46] The decision about preferred alternatives is critical to estimates of the revenue loss from tax-exempt bonds. An entire range of financial and real assets exists with different yields, risk, and degree of preferential taxation. It is not true that the municipal bond purchaser's preferred alternative is always a taxable bond though it is a sound approximation.

[47] Office of Management and Budget, *Economic Report of the President 2011*, Washington, D.C., February 2011.

[48] For example, S. 251 in the 112th Congress would explicitly prohibit the Fed from assisting state and local governments and authorities through purchasing their debt or offering guarantees.

[49] Securities Exchange Act of 1934, Section 15B(d)(1).

[50] Albano, Christine, "Moody's to Weigh Tax-Backed Debt, Pension Liabilities Together," *The Bond Buyer*, January 28, 2011.

In: The Fiscal Strains on State Governments
Editor: Arthur Horváth
ISBN: 978-1-62100-046-4

Chapter 3

REMARKS BY BEN S. BERNANKE, CHAIRMAN, BOARD OF GOVERNORS OF THE FEDERAL RESERVE SYSTEM, AT THE 2011 ANNUAL AWARDS DINNER OF THE CITIZENS BUDGET COMMISSION, "CHALLENGES FOR STATE AND LOCAL GOVERNMENTS"

Ben S. Bernanke

I am pleased to have the opportunity to speak to a group that has such a long and distinguished record in identifying and addressing crucial issues affecting the governments of the city and state of New York. I will focus this evening on a top challenge not only for New York, but also for states and localities across the nation--namely, the imperative of achieving fiscal sustainability in both the short and the long term. I will first discuss the fiscal pressures currently confronting states and localities, then turn to longer-term challenges and opportunities faced by these jurisdictions.

RECENT STATE AND LOCAL FISCAL DEVELOPMENTS

As you know well, the deep recession of 2008 through 2009 and the subsequent slow recovery have battered state and local budgets. As the recession took hold, revenues dropped precipitously, especially at the state level. Driven partly by balanced-budget requirements under their constitutions, many governments have responded by cutting numerous programs and reducing workforces. As necessary as these cuts may have been, they have left some jurisdictions struggling to maintain essential services. The fiscal problems of state and local governments have also had national implications, as their spending cuts and tax increases have been a headwind on the economic recovery. Moreover, concerns about both the current fiscal condition of these governments and their longer-term commitments to provide pensions and health benefits have recently led to strains in municipal bond markets.

The recession's effects on state governments have been substantial. In calendar year 2009, state tax revenues were about 12 percent lower than they had been in 2008; declines in wages, salaries, capital gains, and profits reduced income tax revenues, and sales tax collections dropped along with household and business spending. Reflecting somewhat better economic conditions, state tax revenues for the first nine months of 2010 were 3 percent higher than during the comparable period a year earlier--a relatively modest improvement in comparison to the earlier decline. Meanwhile, on the spending side of the ledger, demand for publicly financed medical care and other public services soared as the economy weakened. Most notably, Medicaid caseloads rose from less than 43 million at the start of the recession in December 2007 to more than 50 million in June 2010--an increase of nearly 18 percent. The experience of New York state has not differed greatly from that of other states: Tax revenues here decreased about 13 percent in 2009 and then rose about 7 percent during the first nine months of 2010. Meanwhile, the state's Medicaid enrollments increased from about 4 million at the end of 2007 to 4-3/4 million in mid-2010--about in line with the national trend.

In contrast to the sharp drop in state tax revenues, local tax revenues across the country have held up relatively well over the past couple of years. In part, this difference reflects localities' greater reliance on property taxes. Changes in real estate values typically feed through to tax assessments and property tax bills with a considerable lag; some jurisdictions have also raised their property tax rates to offset weakness in assessed values. The continued softness in real estate prices, however, does not bode well for local government revenues. Moreover, many localities have been hard hit by reductions in state aid, which in 2008 accounted for about 30 percent of local revenues. Indeed, the fiscal 2011 budgets of more than 20 states contained either outright reductions in local aid, changes to revenue-sharing agreements, or cuts in funding for specific programs that are run by local governments--

such as education for grades kindergarten through 12, road maintenance, and property tax relief.[1]

Assistance from the federal government--mainly through the stimulus grants included in the American Recovery and Reinvestment Act of 2009 (ARRA) and the additional Medicaid and education grants provided last summer--has relieved some of the fiscal pressure on states and localities. In addition, many of them have tapped financial reserves--or "rainy day" funds--and pursued asset sales and other one-time actions to satisfy balanced budget requirements. Nonetheless, many governments have laid off or furloughed workers, frozen salaries, and cut other operating expenses. Job cuts have been especially pronounced at the local level, where payrolls have fallen roughly 350,000, or more than 2 percent, over the past 2-1/2 years; nearly half of the loss of local jobs has been in education.

In addition, state and local governments have cut their capital expenditures. To be sure, construction of highways and transportation facilities has been well maintained over the past couple of years, partly because of the infrastructure grants and the Build America Bond program provided under the ARRA. But outlays for the construction of schools to serve students in grades kindergarten through 12 now stand about 30 percent below their pre-recession level. One might ask why states and localities are choosing to reduce capital expenditures, as these expenditures provide employment and economic benefits while typically not being subject to balanced budget requirements. One reason is that some projects are funded at least partially out of operating budgets and thus must compete with Medicaid and other high-priority programs for scarce dollars. Another is that a sizable share of debt service payments on the bonds used to finance capital projects comes from operating budgets, further limiting the flexibility and willingness of governments to undertake new infrastructure projects. Finally, starting new capital projects may be difficult to justify politically in a period of general austerity.

At least a few states have raised taxes and fees to address budget shortfalls. As you know, in 2009 the state of New York enacted a package of revenue measures that included a temporary surcharge on taxes paid by high-income individuals. California also raised income and sales taxes that year. And after having seen its credit rating sink to among the lowest in the nation, Illinois recently implemented a sizable increase in income taxes.

Despite the many difficult adjustments to date, state and local fiscal repair is far from complete, and governors, mayors, and legislators will confront more tough decisions as they develop their budgets for fiscal year 2012. Although the economy is recovering, it is still operating well below potential and unemployment remains high. Stimulus grants from the federal government are winding down this year and will largely have ended by 2012. Demands on Medicaid and other social service programs will likely remain elevated. Moreover, reserve funds are low, and the list of unused one-time fixes has been substantially depleted.

Nonetheless, some positive developments have emerged lately. For example, closest to home, Mayor Bloomberg announced last month that the city of New York has revised up its estimates of tax revenue for both the current and upcoming fiscal years. As I noted earlier, state revenues nationwide have been rising recently, and states are generally reporting that collections are running in line with--and, in some cases, a bit ahead of--expectations. Accordingly, considerably fewer states are facing midyear budget gaps that will need to be addressed before the end of the current fiscal year than the 40 or so that reported such gaps in 2009 and 2010.

Much will depend on the continuation of the economic recovery. If the economy continues to strengthen at about the pace projected by the Federal Reserve and many private forecasters, states and localities may start to get a little breathing space. Tax collections will rise with income and spending, and the use of Medicaid and other income support programs should ease as the labor market improves. However, because the pace of near-term economic growth expected by most forecasters is relatively modest given the depth of the downturn, some time will likely be required before state and local fiscal conditions return to something approximating normal.

Continued evidence that states and localities are addressing fiscal shortfalls should help calm the municipal bond market. Generally, that market seems to be functioning reasonably well. Around the turn of the year, though, investor concerns about the fiscal situations of many governments, including those of some populous states, resulted in increased yields on municipal bonds relative to Treasury bonds as well as a widening of credit default swap spreads for a number of states. Fortunately, although these measures of risk in the municipal bond market remain elevated, they have been looking somewhat better recently, presumably reflecting expectations of continuing improvement in the finances of states and localities. The Federal Reserve will continue to monitor the municipal bond market closely.

LONGER-RUN FISCAL CHALLENGES FOR STATES AND LOCALITIES

Although my focus thus far has been on the near term, state and local governments are also confronting some difficult fiscal challenges in the longer term. Indeed, with the retirement of public employees who are part of the baby-boom generation and the continued rise in health-care costs, meeting obligations for pension and retiree health-care expenses will become increasingly difficult for many states and localities. Estimates of state and local governments' unfunded pension liabilities for the nation as a whole span a wide range, with some researchers putting the figure in the neighborhood of $2 trillion to $3 trillion.[2] Some governments are beginning to take difficult steps to address this problem, although their ability to change plan provisions is limited by the strong legal protection (including, in some states, constitutional protection) accorded to accrued pension benefits of public employees in many jurisdictions.[3]

State and local governments also will have to address the burgeoning costs of retiree health benefits. Estimates of these costs are subject to substantially greater uncertainty than are those for pension liabilities, largely because of the difficulty inherent in projecting overall health-care costs decades into the future. In addition, retiree health plans generally do not have the same degree of explicit protection as do pensions and thus may be more subject to change. With these uncertainties in mind, the prospective costs of providing retiree health benefits--though certainly consequential--appear to be somewhat smaller than unfunded pension liabilities. For example, one recent estimate suggests that state governments have a collective liability of almost $600 billion for retiree health benefits.[4]

Not all of the longer-term issues facing state and local fiscal authorities involve closing budget gaps. For example, in light of the recent experience, an important question is whether anything can be done to reduce the sensitivity of state and local budgets to the business cycle. As the past couple of years have shown, the balanced- budget rules under which most states operate can force sharp cuts in services and increases in taxes during recessions, which is just the time when many people in the state are economically most vulnerable. Moreover, the instability in funding streams and tax rates associated with the business cycle can impede planning by both the public and the private sectors.

By and large, the evidence suggests that balanced-budget rules provide valuable fiscal discipline for states, and I do not advocate eliminating them.[5]

However, even with these rules in place, the question remains whether the effects of the business cycle on state budgets can be mitigated in the future. One strategy used by many governments is to build up a rainy day fund during good economic times. Measured as a percent of general fund expenditures, the aggregate reserve-fund balances for all state governments stood at a record 11-1/2 percent at the end of fiscal 2006. These comparatively high reserve-fund balances have lessened the severity of spending cuts or tax increases in many states during the past couple of years. However, given the depth of the recession, even these historically high balances proved insufficient to fully buffer the budgets of most states. Thus, governments may wish to revisit their criteria for accumulating and using fiscal reserves. Building an adequate reserve fund during good times may not be politically popular, but doing so can pay off during bad times as well as lessen the tendency to overspend when times are good.

In principle, some smoothing of expenditures over good and bad times could also take place through the capital budget. In particular, maintaining or even increasing the pace of construction spending when the economy is weak could add valuable infrastructure and provide local jobs; it may even allow a government to get more "bang for the buck" because of increased competition among private contractors when demand is slack. Voters and policymakers may understandably be reluctant to approve new bond issues and take on additional costs for debt payments in a period of fiscal and economic stress, but they might be less reluctant if governments were to accumulate larger rainy day funds and assign a higher priority to tapping them for infrastructure purposes in times of economic weakness.

Another development that has compounded the difficulties faced by many state governments is that their revenues--always sensitive to economic conditions--appear to have become even more tied to the economy over time. One reason for this greater sensitivity is that capital income, which tends to vary substantially more than wage and salary income, has become an increasingly important source of state personal income taxes.[6] Also, sales taxes may have become more cyclical because of an increasing tendency to exempt certain necessities, for which demand is relatively more stable. As state legislatures review their tax systems, they may wish to consider steps to enhance the cyclical stability of their revenue streams. Of course, many considerations enter into tax policy, including the fairness of the code, the support it provides for economic growth and development, and the level of administrative and compliance costs.

Budget balance and budget stability are important fiscal issues. In the long run, though, the most important fiscal issue is whether the structure and composition of the government budget best serves the public interest. Certainly, most people would support the goal of fostering healthy economic growth. Government can contribute to this objective in a number of ways. One critical means is by ensuring an adequate investment in human capital--that is, in the knowledge and skills of our people. No economy can succeed without a high-quality workforce, particularly in an age of globalization and technical change. Cost-effective K-12 and post-secondary schooling are crucial to building a better workforce, but they are only part of the story. Research increasingly has shown the benefits of early childhood education and efforts to promote the lifelong acquisition of skills for both individuals and the economy as a whole. The payoffs of early childhood programs can be especially high.[7] For instance, preschool programs for disadvantaged children have been shown to increase high school graduation rates.[8] Because high school graduates have higher earnings, pay more taxes, and are less likely to use public health programs, investing in such programs can pay off even from the narrow perspective of state budgets; of course, the returns to the overall economy and to the individuals themselves are much greater.

Additionally, in a dynamic economy in which job requirements are evolving more rapidly than ever, individuals already in the workforce need opportunities to improve their skills throughout their lives. There are many ways to provide such opportunities. For example, community colleges and vocational schools train and retrain workers, often in close collaboration with private employers, and in many cases they perform this function at a relatively low cost. Although helping workers acquire up-to-date skills is always important, it is especially critical now, when long spells of unemployment are threatening the longer-term employability and productivity of many.

CONCLUSION

Tonight I have highlighted some of the fiscal challenges faced by elected officials, both in New York and in other regions. In the past few years, the weak economy has significantly reduced government revenues, which in turn has forced governments to make difficult decisions on spending and taxes. An improving economy should help, but state and local finances will remain under pressure for some time. Moreover, states and localities are facing difficult longer-run issues related to pension and health-related expenses for their retired employees. These challenges are daunting indeed, but meeting them will be essential to ensuring that our resilient and dynamic economy delivers rising living standards to the citizens of New York and to our nation as a whole.

End Notes

[1] See National Governors Association and the National Association of State Budget Officers (2010), *The Fiscal Survey of States* (Washington: NASBO, Fall).

[2] See Alicia H. Munnell, Richard W. Kopcke, Jean-Pierre Aubry, and [2] See Alicia H. Munnell, Richard W. Kopcke, Jean-Pierre Aubry, and Laura Quinby (2010), *Valuing Liabilities in State and Local Plans* (Chestnut Hill, Mass.: Center for Retirement Research at Boston College, June), http://crr.bc.edu/briefs/valuing_liabilities_in_state_and_local_plans.html; and Robert NovyMarx and Joshua D. Rauh (forthcoming), "Public Pension Promises: How Big Are They and What Are They Worth?" *Journal of Finance*.

[3] See Jeffrey R. Brown and David W. Wilcox (2009), "Discounting State and Local Pension Liabilities," *American Economic Review*, vol. 99 (May), pp. 53 8-42. It should be noted that *future* pension accruals generally seem to be accorded a lower level of protection.

[4] See Pew Center on the States (2010), *The Trillion Dollar Gap: Underfunded State Retirement Systems and the Road to Reform* (Washington: PCS, February), *www.pewcenteronthestates .org/report_detail.aspx?id=56695.*

[5] See, for example, James M. Poterba (1995), "Balanced Budget Rules and Fiscal Policy: Evidence from the States," *National Tax Journal*, vol. 48 (3), pp. 329-3 6.

[6] See Richard Mattoon and Leslie McGranahan (2008), "Revenue Bubbles and Structural Deficits: What's a State to Do?" Working Paper No. 2008-15 (Chicago: Federal Reserve Bank of Chicago, July), www.chicagofed.org/webpages/publications/working_papers/2008 /wp_15.cfm and David L. Sjoquist and Sally Wallace (2003), "Capital Gains: Its Recent, Varied, and Growing (?) Impact on State Revenues," *State Tax Notes*, August 18, www.taxpolicycenter.org/publications/url.cfm?ID=1000613.

[7] For example, see the work of the Human Capital Research Collaborative, a joint project of the University of Minnesota and the Federal Reserve Bank of Minneapolis, at www.humancapitalrc.org.

[8] See, for example, Henry M. Levin, Clive Belfield, Peter Muennig, Cecilia Rouse, Barbara Wolfe, and Nathan Tefft (2007), "The Public Returns to Public Educational Investments in African American Males," *Economics of Education Review*, vol. 26, pp. 700-09.

CHAPTER SOURCES

The Following chapters have been previousily published:

Chapter 1 – This is an edited, reformatted and augmented version of Congressional Research Service Report R41773, dated April 31, 2011.
Chapter 2 – This is an edited, reformatted and augmented version of Congressional Research Service Report R41735, dated April 28, 2011.
Chapter 3 – These remakrs were delivered as testimony given on March 11, 2011, Ben S. Bernanke, Chairman, Board of Governors of theFederal Reserve System before the Citizens Budget Commission.

INDEX

H

I

J

K

L

M

N

O

P

R

S

T